UNITED
AGAINST
RACISM

UNITED
AGAINST
RACISM

CHURCHES FOR CHANGE

NATIONAL COUNCIL OF CHURCHES OF CHRIST IN THE USA

National Council of Churches of Christ in the USA
Washington, DC

Cover by Kingdom Graphic Design LLC.

Scripture quotations are from the New Revised Standard Version Bible, copyright 1989 by the Division of Christian Education of the National Council of the Churches of Christ in the USA. Used by permission.

CONTENTS

An Invitation to the Churches

Grace to you and peace from God our Father and the Lord Jesus Christ.

As I greet you, my friends, I echo the words and sentiments of the Apostle Paul as he celebrated the Romans in his letter to the church at Rome:

First, I thank my God through Jesus Christ for all of you, because your faith is proclaimed throughout the world. For God, whom I serve with my spirit by announcing the gospel of his Son, is my witness that without ceasing I remember you always in my prayers.

—Romans 1:7b

On the night prior to his assassination, Dr. Martin Luther King Jr. reflected on how he and others faced such a vital time in their current situation. Dr. King commented that if he could live in any period—in Egypt as the Israelites crossed the Red Sea, in ancient Greece to stand on Mount Olympus, or in the heyday of the Roman Empire—he would choose the present.

I trust that we too have this confidence. We live in a challenging time, to be sure, but there is no better time to live and no better people than we to face these challenges! We are equipped, fortified, and prepared by God's grace to meet and surmount the challenges that await us. Through the prayers that bind us, the goals that unite us, and the surpassing belief in the ultimate and victorious resurrection power of the Risen Lord we serve, our common witness will prevail. In this faith we progress, assured in the words of Julian of Norwich: "I understood that we may laugh, to comfort ourselves and rejoice in God, because the devil is overcome."[1]

---

1   Julian of Norwich and Lisa E. Dahill, ed., *40-Day Journey with Julian of Norwich* (Minneapolis, MN: Augsburg Books, 2008), 40.

The indispensable and inescapable element of our unity will be prayer. Prayer, joined by all God's people, is the most effective means we have of achieving unity, overcoming any obstacle, or healing the broken bonds of our nation as well as our individual and uniquely diverse communities. As we pray and worship together, we realize we are bound by this commonality of our faith, and we will discover that Walter Brueggemann is correct when he observes, "The intent of the liturgy is to put the residence of YHWH (and so the claims of the urban establishment) beyond the reach of historical contingency."[2]

It was in 1517 that Martin Luther placed his treatise, Disputation on the Power and Efficacy of Indulgences—or, as the document is better known, the Ninety-Five Theses—on the door of the castle church in Wittenberg, Germany. In an act similar to what may now be a Facebook or social media post, Luther intended to invite discussion and debate among academics, scholars, and thinkers about the current practices and future reality of the church. Did his post create controversy? Certainly! But it also set in motion forces that we believe were guided by the Holy Spirit, forces that would not be stopped as the church of Jesus Christ moved inexorably, even if at times reluctantly, toward that promised Kingdom of God here on earth.

Let us now take on this challenge as churches united against racism to face in every way the obstacles to the fulfilment of that same promised Kingdom of God. Guided by the "Vision and Objectives for the ACT Now: Unite to End Racism" work of the National Council of Churches, we recognize indeed that *this is the moment*: "The World Council of Churches as part of its 'Pilgrimage of Justice and Peace' has called the U.S. churches to grapple with issues of racism particularly facing the African American community."[3] This we will do unflinchingly and without compromise, sure that, as the great pastor and hymn writer Charles Albert Tindley wrote,

---

2   Walter Brueggemann, *Reality, Grief, Hope: Three Urgent Prophetic Tasks* (Grand Rapids, MI: William B. Eerdmans, 2014), 11.

3   From the "Vision and Objectives for the Truth and Racial Justice Initiative of the National Council of Churches," 2017.

Harder yet may be the fight;
Right may often yield to might;
Wickedness a while may reign;
Satan's cause may seem to gain.
There is a God that rules above,
With hand of power and heart of love,
If I am right, he'll fight my battle,
I shall have peace someday.[4]

Yours for justice, mercy, and peace,
The Right Reverend W. Darin Moore
Chair of the National Council of the Churches of Christ in the USA
Presiding Bishop of the Mid-Atlantic Episcopal
District, African Methodist Episcopal Zion Church

---

4   Charles Albert Tindley, ca. 1906, "Beams of Heaven as I Go."

INTRODUCTION

MRS. JACQUELYN DUPONT WALKER
AND REV. DR. JOHN C. DORHAUER

After almost twelve months of prayer, pondering, and preparation, the National Council of the Churches of Christ's thirty-eight-member communions (often denoted by the term *denominations* in common usage) are preparing to take a faith walk. The journey is to ACT Now: Unite to End Racism. The prayer and hope of ACT Now is to *awaken, confront,* and *transform* our churches and nation into becoming a nation united as one when it comes to standing against racism and for Christians to experience and embody an inclusive and beloved community. This is what we mean by authentic Christianity. Without hesitation, we assert that racism is a sin that continues to tear the fabric of the United States of America. Though other places in the world struggle with discrimination, biases, and government-sponsored injustices, we focus on where we "do" ministry—this is our watch! For each church and Christian community, where we live, learn, work, and play is the context and focus of where we serve. It matters that we have been complicit by our silence and weakest of actions. It matters that we are seeing the rebirth of aggressive acts of hatred and violence against people simply because of their race and ethnicity.[1] It matters that our churches talk about this sin yet nurture and allow it to continue without challenge in hundreds of thousands of local congregations and community gatherings.

This is our watch! This faith walk is not just the right thing to do; it is the core of who and what we are called to be—authentic, faithful followers of Jesus. It must not be an addition to an already crowded agenda but the very essence of claiming the voice of the Church of Jesus Christ. We must

---

1   See the Southern Poverty Law Center's "Hate Map," https://www.splcenter.org/hate
    -map.

discover solutions and help people find personal empowerment in their faith walk—to face bigotry, call out injustice, and stand, even if it finds us standing alone. It is urgent that we find solutions and sustain our efforts to end racism now. Who benefits? Without fear of contradiction, the world benefits!

The time is now, as signaled by the United Nations' decade-long commitment to people of African descent. "In proclaiming this decade, the international community is recognizing that people of African descent represent a distinct group whose human rights must be promoted and protected. Around 200 million people identifying themselves as being of African descent live in the Americas. Many millions more live in other parts of the world, outside of the African continent."[2]

Further confirmation comes from the World Council of Churches (WCC). Two years ago, the WCC toured the US and witnessed atrocities regarding our ongoing manifestations of white power, white privilege, and white supremacy. They issued a challenge to the National Council of Churches of Christ in the USA (NCC) to act—to utilize its agency as an instrument for change to address the festering wound of racism in America.

Rev. King Solomon Dupont, at his retirement service during the annual meeting of his judicatory in Florida, said in the 1970s as he was retiring from active resistance work, "I knew I would leave some struggles, but not the same ole ones."[3] After more than sixty-seven years as a force for racial equity and justice, the National Council of the Churches of Christ in the USA understands that activist's cry of woe. We are struck by the continuing threat to the body of Christ and our collective rejection of the Holy Spirit's persistent push to end the sin of racism. Christian churches, let us take up Prophet Isaiah's challenge to abandon our false worship for authentic worship of God.[4] Let us vow to use this time so that the struggles we leave for future generations are not the sins or struggles of the past.

---

2   United Nations, http://www.un.org/en/events/africandescentdecade/.

3   Rev. King Solomon Dupont, cochair of the Tallahassee Civic Association, who led the Tallahassee Bus Boycott in 1956.

4   Isa. 58.

Intent of This Resource

The Church of Jesus Christ aspires and strives to be an inclusive, beloved community. For this to be achieved, Christians must become agents of love, safety, and openness toward the "other" as much as people are instinctively loving, trusting, and open to those with whom they share likes, dislikes, and other characteristics. Authentic Christianity is personal *and* it's relational. Authentic Christianity requires the loving inclusion of all God's creation. An inclusive, beloved community is a community free from racism. *United Against Racism* is a call to an authentic Christianity, a religion that strives to become God's inclusive, beloved community. It summons Christians to pray, think, and act to end racism. This resource aims to support churches, communions, and those who endeavor to share the journey of the Christian faith in the pursuit of an unfinished agenda to embody a more excellent way of racial equity. Racial equity and the Christian faith are inextricably tied together.

While reconciliation is a sign of an inclusive, beloved community, our task is to discern the truth and work that truth into our lives. Truth-telling is a key pillar of the truth and reconciliation process. For it to be inviting and generative, we believe it is necessary to frame "truth-telling" in terms of "dialogue" and "conversation" more so than "telling," which connotes or emphasizes one-way communication. Leonard Swidler writes, "Dialogue is a two-way communication between persons who hold significantly differing views on a subject, with the purpose of learning more truth about the subject from the other. . . . Dialogue must include a common understanding that no one side has a monopoly on the truth of any given subject. . . . The general goal of dialogue is for each side to learn and to change accordingly."[5]

In our world today, the idea of "truth" as universal or particular, constant or ever changing, is debatable. Swidler provides an alternative to views of "truth" being either "true" or "false." The *truth* we strive to know and make known is "related to the historical context, intentionality,

---

5 Leonard Swidler, "Understanding Dialogue," in *Interfaith Dialogue at the Grass Roots* (Philadelphia: Ecumenical Press, 2008), 11–13.

perspective, language, and interpretation" of groups, communities, and their policies and practices. In this context, the truth we seek to understand is not absolute, and it is not relative; it is relational.

This resource is asking us to do the real work of our Christian faith. We must confront racism head on through a series of conversations, prayers, reflections, and group activities and the sharing of stories. Our goal is to help us all not miss the mark this time. Our goal is to not substitute words of reconciliation for peace with justice. Our goal is to do the work of justice through racial equity as God's mandate. Our goal is to use pedagogically sound approaches that encourage critical reflection and action, inspire and call others to join the National Council of Churches in this just and noble cause, and deliver a resource that affirms the diversity of the ecumenical community and is valuable and applicable to the Church, our nation, and the world.

How to Use This Resource
This resource is not designed to be read like a novel from cover to cover. Instead, it is a resource for working and living relationally for racial justice. It offers prayers, thoughts, and reflections for use by individuals, small groups, congregations, and communities who strive to express and embody authentic Christianity. For churches, this resource can serve as a tool for conversation surrounding truth-telling and racial equity in small or large group settings. For individuals, this resource can serve as a source for deep theological reflection on social relations and how the way society is arranged helps and hinders us from living in community with others. For faith communities operating at regional and national levels, the prayers and thoughts prompt reform and transformative action about how an inclusive, beloved community calls Christians to examine policies and change priorities for achieving racial equity and ending racism.

Brief Overview
The resource is divided into eleven themes, each with "Key Terms," "Narrative and prayers," "Think about It. Talk about It," "Engage," and

"Go Deeper. Read More" sections. Following the last theme, "What Will You Do?," there is a section, "Learning Practices for People of Faith." This section is provided to help persons and groups wanting to extend the conversations to do so in greater depth.

Mary E. Hess offers a thought-provoking framework for understanding the current brokenness of our nation and the contribution religious educational practices can lend in the service of reconciliation. Hess creatively puts together a view on how digital media can be employed to help today's learners re-engage with views, symbols, and understandings of Christian faith that promote an inclusive, beloved community as an expression of authentic Christianity. Hess's educational methods and recommended uses of digital media invite participants to reflect on what in their own experiences resonates and is dissonant with those of scripture and tradition.

United Against Racism concludes with an extensive list of resources that pastors, educators, and concerned leaders can draw on to support their growth and that of their congregation. Throughout the project, our aim is to undergird Christian communities in their work of building inclusive, beloved communities that express and embody love, safety, and openness as an antidote against racism. We declare that racism and every barrier of exclusion exist only in opposition to the reign of God and the life Jesus lived, the cause for which he died, and the purpose for which God raised him to live forevermore.

Mourning the Trauma

Rev. Karen Georgia A. Thompson
United Church of Christ

They have treated the wound of my people carelessly, saying, "Peace, peace," when there is no peace.

—Jeremiah 6:14

Key Terms

Prejudice is a personal attitude toward other people based on a categorical judgment about their physical characteristics, such as race or ethnic origin.

Race is described by sociologists Neil J. Smelser, William Julius Wilson, and Faith Mitchell as "a social category based on the identification of (1) a physical marker transmitted through reproduction and (2) individual, group, and cultural attributes associated with that marker. In this way, *race* is both a form of ethnicity and distinguishable from other forms of ethnicity."[1]

Racism is racial prejudice plus power. Racism is the intentional or unintentional use of power to isolate, separate, and exploit others. This use of power is based on a belief in superior racial origin, identity, or supposed racial characteristics. Racism confers certain privileges on and defends the dominant group, which in turn sustains and perpetuates racism. Both consciously and unconsciously, racism is enforced and maintained by the legal, cultural, religious, educational, economic, political, and military institutions of societies.

---

1   Neil J. Smelser, William Julius Wilson, and Faith Mitchell, eds., introduction to *America Becoming: Racial Trends and Their Consequences*, vol. 1. (Washington, DC: National Academy Press, 2001), 3.

Trauma refers to the cause and effect of an injury or wound produced by tragedy, harm, or violence. Traumatic experiences, either physical or psychological, can have lasting emotional consequences.

UN-sanitized

I tried to teach my sons what my parents
attempted to teach me
they tried to keep me safe
they did their best to warn me
there are rules, they said
rules to be upheld
these rules unwritten
these rules filled my head
these rules kept me in check
institutionally chained
these rules kept me sanitized with these rules
there was shaming and pain

keep your mouth shut
avert your eyes
hands on the wheel
no moves that surprise
no fancy cars
no fancy clothes
learn your place
keep your disdain off your face
I played by the rules
I taught my kids
be polite,
to follow those rules

smile when you are upset
keep your hands where they can be seen
bring your anger home,

don't show your rage
in the streets
don't run after dark
dress the right way
don't walk in a pack
that guarantees
you stay off the front page

the more polite I am
the more that boot presses into my neck
my anger must be kept in check
gloriously sanitized
while your ill-will and hate
is fed like spit on a plate
the open hatred you display
the fearless way you name your disdain
I must swallow like a pill
as my words get stuffed in my throat
again

to not be that angry Black woman
I must keep my mouth shut
nod my head
shrink into your back room
well, here's the news
I was never one to cower
I will no longer de-sanitize myself
in the confines of my shower
in an attempt to keep you satisfied
when you are
so wrong

the hot water cannot remove the staining
of your words

the soap cannot cleanse
the rage that you provoke
I am choking to death every day
on the anger I swallow
every time I go out

go do your work
re-educate yourself
you are not better because you said
so get your dirty boot
off my neck
I will no longer "watch my words"
I will no longer fear your stinking jails
I will no longer allow you to define me as unsafe
my un-sanitized self you will meet today

with your guns, your privilege, your pale
I afforded you grace
the scriptures you used said that was my place
I suggest you not confuse me with the Holy
or use my race as some deep disgrace
my anger you will meet
I will walk on able feet
rather than sit and swallow that garbage that you mete
so step back slowly out of my space
you will not determine my worth
you will not determine my words
you will not write my script
I will be heard
the fear is gone
the revolution has begun
remember
you heard it here first

I have too many experiences of racism, too many memories of racist attitudes and discrimination. I vividly remember my earliest memory of being treated differently because of my race, which occurred when I was about six years old. On that occasion, I was in the school yard playing. Ours was the context of a colonized island in the Caribbean and a predominantly African-descendant population. Yet even there, that one white male child of the same age defined my existence the day he threw a pebble from the gravel in the yard and hit me in my head.

I remember the moment that the stone made contact with my skin, just above my hairline. I remember the blood. I remember being taken to the school infirmary so they could stop the bleeding. Even more lasting is the memory that he was never punished for injuring my person, nor was he held accountable for the pain he caused me that day. Because of the color of his skin, he was exempt from the rules of our small black school. His parents were missionaries, there to bring the good news of Jesus to the Caribbean island.

I experienced racism from every category of place and space where my feet trod during my lifetime. I find that I am still surprised by the places and the collection of racist incidents and encounters that I continue to amass, knowing and refusing to believe that racism and prejudice are normative. I want to believe that there are safe places and sacred places where all are welcome and all are free, yet I continue to encounter people who have no love or respect for my person of this black skin I occupy.

I am an ordained minister in a mainline Protestant Christian denomination. I have availed myself of educational opportunities. I hold two master's degrees, and I am working on a doctorate. I made choices for my education and for the education of my children, and over the years, I lived in neighborhoods that I thought would be safe for my children and for me. None of this has diminished my exposure (or theirs) to racism and racist experiences or shielded my family from the trauma of racist people and the toxicity they spew.

Today was one of those days I had to remind myself that regardless of the ways in which I try to insulate myself and how I think I have equipped my children to live their lives, the color of our skin means that we are deemed to be unsafe and results in spaces where we are present being unsafe for us: schools, airports, airplanes, markets, stores—even in my own home. Recently came the reminder that the church is also an unsafe space for people of African descent. The church is unsafe for me. My experiences of racism in the church continue to be traumatic and contrary to the gospel message and the love that Jesus calls us to.

Today was a sunny, crisp February morning in Chicago, and I was excited about finishing the meeting I was attending and going home. I readied myself and took the elevator to the lobby for checkout. As I crossed the lobby, I stopped to say good morning to colleagues standing in the lobby. We were all there for the same meeting. One, a white male, responded to my greeting with, "When I saw you coming through the lobby, pushing your suitcase, I thought you were the cleaning woman." He is in a prominent position in another mainline denomination, an individual who is well respected, a theologian. The second person, a white female, said nothing. I walked away.

I wonder about my grandchildren and the world they will see as they grow older. They are now one, two, and five years old. Will their experiences be the same? I am angry! I feel the rush of blood boiling in my veins. I feel frustrated that I now have conversations with my sons that mirror the racism I encountered and they experienced in the public-school system as children.

I worry about the millions of African-descendant children passing through our educational systems when I hear about the racist experiences my five-year-old grandson is already having in school. I am angry at the knowledge that there appears to be no end in sight to the wounding of people and the increasing scars that are present for African-descendant people. I am angry that the church finds a way to be silent in the face of the litany of experiences of African-descendant people.

I am tired, and yet I keep fighting. I am tired of having words hurled at me carelessly. I am tired of the ways in which white privilege and white supremacy continue to promulgate even in the church. I am tired for generations to come. I am tired for generations past. I am tired, but I cannot and will not embrace the weariness because I do not want my grandchildren to experience the brutality of racism in any form. I continue to advocate for a just world for all.

I came to the realization that trauma is real in environments that do not promote or provide safety for all people and, more specifically, for me. There is violence in the manifestations of racism, whether it be overt attacks or subtle microaggressions. This violence induces trauma, anger, and frustration.

Eight months after the incident in that hotel lobby in Chicago, I had to return to a meeting of the same group. I had a hard time getting myself together to go. The packing was slow. I felt ill, but there were no symptoms to identify. I motivated myself to get to the airport, nursing this undefined unwellness. On the plane, I remembered the incident in the hotel lobby.

My body remembered the trauma I attempted to forget. I decided then, I will no longer go to places where I experienced the trauma of racism and retraumatize myself, especially when those places, like the church, should offer safety.

AUTHENTIC CARE TOWARD GOD'S PEOPLE

REV. DR. CHRISTOPHER L. ZACHARIAS
JOHN WESLEY AFRICAN METHODIST EPISCOPAL
CHURCH (AME) ZION CHURCH

Lord Jesus, I am reminded of Your teachings to the Pharisees and Your disciples of the character of a Good Shepherd, one who protects, cares for, loves, and cherishes the sheep. In the same manner, help Your body of believers to do the same by protecting Your sheep from hired hands of persons (lawyers, judges, police officers, politicians, religious leaders, government workers, and others) who will and may abandon their sworn responsibilities of proper care for all people.

Help us mend the mental, physical, emotional, and spiritual wounds of Your sheep through appropriate ministries that undergird assistance of Your sheep's social woes. Help us provide ministries of feeding the hungry, clothing the poor, educating and assisting under-achieved and underprivileged children, and so much more.

Lord, help us be visible examples of a Good Samaritan who sees the needs of Your people. Let us stop and minister to those needs and, if we are unable to address them, then assist them with resources and persons who can address their needs. Let us not walk by those who are hurting by homelessness, afflicted by unemployment, and emotion-ally wounded by depression.

Grant us the compassion to lend a hand that will help allevi-ate their conditions, assure them that we authentically care, and assist the less fortunate toward a better quality of life. Your words ring true: "Truly I tell you, just as you did it to one of the least of theses who are members of my family, you did it to me."[2] In Jesus's name, Amen.

PRAYER TO BECOME AGENTS OF LOVE

REV. VERNON SHANNON
ECUMENICAL AND GOVERNMENTAL REPRESENTATIVE
PHILADELPHIA AND BALTIMORE AME ZION CHURCH CONFERENCE

O God, our heavenly Father, You have made us of one blood, all nations to dwell upon the earth. You created the human family to be as one with each other, "to do justly, to love mercy and to walk humbly with our God."[3] You gave us prophets to admonish us to "let

---

2   Matt. 24:40.
3   Mic. 6:8.

justice roll down like waters and righteousness like an ever-flowing stream."[4]

We confess, O God, that instead of recognizing and celebrating our oneness, we have divided ourselves into races, classes, colors, and nationalities. We have even declared that some of your children are inferior and others are superior.

We have witnessed the brutality, the lynching, the hatred, the prejudice, the segregation, and the denial of freedom and justice for all.

The cancer of racism is gnawing away the moral fabric of our nation. Everywhere we look, we see race against race and the denial of the sacredness of every human personality.

O God, we pray that you will open our eyes and heal the brokenness of our nation and world. Your Son Jesus prayed "that we might all be one." Help us know that we are one, and help us overcome racism, bigotry, and hatred. Help us be instruments of your love so that where there is hatred, we might bring love.

We thank you, O God, for individuals and organizations like the NAACP, the National Council of Churches in America, and others whose efforts are to end racism, bring in the day of brotherhood and sisterhood, and end the night of wrong.

Hear our prayer, O God, and hasten the day when we shall overcome racism in our nation and world.

In the name of Jesus, our Lord, who is the Christ, we make this request. Amen.

---

4   Amos 5:24.

CONFESSIONS

REV. SHELDON W. SORGE, PhD
GENERAL MINISTER
PRESBYTERY OF PITTSBURGH, PRESBYTERIAN CHURCH (USA)

This prayer is based on a church confession adopted by the Presbyterian Church amid the unrest of the 1960s. It is one of twelve historic church confessions that the Presbyterian Church includes in its constitution. This prayer is suitable for use in worship as a confession of sin, or it can be used as an affirmation of faith by substituting the second person "you" with "God" and adjusting verbs accordingly. The full text of the Confession of 1967 is available in *The Book of Confessions.*[5]

Righteous God,

Your reconciling work in Jesus Christ and the ministry of reconciliation to which he calls us is the heart of the gospel in all places and times. Though he is present with us by the power of the Holy Spirit to continue and complete his mission of reconciliation, we have resisted the Spirit by refusing to do all within our own power to be reconciled to people different from ourselves. Despite the gravity and cost of Jesus's work to reconcile us to God and one another, we have tolerated and even nurtured separation in the church along lines of racial ethnic heritage. While all humanity stands under the scrutiny of your righteous judgment, no one is more subject to that judgment than those who assume they are guiltless before you or morally superior to others.

Yet you love us. When we oppose you, you express your love in wrath. We acknowledge that the racism that still infects our society is truly hateful, whether we perpetrate it actively or submit to it passively. Whether by exclusion, domination, or patronization of those

---

5   *The Book of Confessions: The Constitution of the Presbyterian Church (U.S.A.) Part 1* (Louisville, KY: Presbyterian Church [USA], 2016), 299–306.

with another racial heritage, we have grievously sinned against you and against one another. We deserve only judgment yet dare to place our hope in the grace you give us through Jesus's work of reconciliation on our behalf.

You have called us to labor for the abolition of all racial discrimination and to minister to those injured by it. Enable us by your Holy Spirit to uphold those of races other than our own wherever you place us to serve your mission in the world: in employment, housing, education, leisure, marriage, family, church, and the exercise of political rights. With an urgency born of the hope of your coming kingdom, we devote ourselves fully to the work of reconciliation in our world, undaunted by disappointment or defeat. In Jesus's name and for his sake, Amen.

Think about It. Talk about It.

Have you or someone you know ever experienced bias, discrimination, exclusion, or rejection based on your or their race or ethnicity?
How did you or they feel?
What did you or they do?
What do you believe should be the "ought" in such situations? How *ought* Christians respond?

Engage

David A. Hardcastle and Patricia R. Powers wrote that a part of community responsibility is to know the whole picture, while community credibility comes from knowing a cross-section of the people and their stories.[6]

1. Assemble a team of four to eight persons from different racial and ethnic backgrounds. Identify a community where the majority of residents are people of color. Recruit one or more church leaders

---

6   David A. Hardcastle and Patricia R. Powers, *Community Practice: Theories and Skills for Social Workers*, 2nd ed. (New York: Oxford University Press, 2004), 145.

in that community to help you discover, document, and discuss a traumatic episode or event that residents perceive to be based on race. Use the following questions to inform your work:

- What kind of neighborhood would you say this is?
- What are some stories most people in this area could tell us?
- What are good and bad points about living in this area?
- Has this area experienced any racial tragedies in the past one to three years that people still remember or talk about?
- How is the tragedy influencing how they now live?

2. Following the discovery and documentation, ask the group the following:
- How do you feel about what you learned?
- Who controls the resources that could help alleviate the pain?
- Who has access to those power brokers?

3. Consider and explore how your congregation(s) might respond.

Go Deeper. Read More.

Boyce, Gregory. "The Execution of Michael Brown: A Barbershop Analysis of a Police-Murder." *Examiner*, December 2, 2014. http://www.examiner.com/article/the-execution-of-michael-brown-a-barbershop-analysis.

Wallis, Jim. "Racism: America's Original Sin." Series: Remembering Trayvon, *Sojourners*, July 29, 2013. Accessed February 3, 2016. https://sojo.net/articles/remembering-trayvon/racism-americas-original-sin#sthash.JMvOMlA1.V6tmiqY2.dpuf.

BROKEN TRUST

RACISM, WHITE PRIVILEGE,
AND MISUNDERSTANDING

*If you see in a province the oppression of the poor and the violation of
justice and right, do not be amazed at the matter; for the high official
is watched by a higher, and there are yet higher ones over them.*
                                                    —Ecclesiastes 5:8

Key Terms

DIALOGUE is a "two-way communication between persons who hold significantly differing views on a subject, with the purpose of learning more
truth about the subject from the other. . . . Dialogue must include a
common understanding that no one side has a monopoly on the truth
on any given subject."[1]

TRUST, the reliance upon the words, promises, integrity, strength, or ability
of others, is foundational for any relationship or the establishment of
community. Through broken promises, betrayal of commitments, or the
violation of values, trust is lost.

TRUTH-TELLING refers to the moral obligation to be honest while recognizing
that one's view is limited to her or his place in the world.

The Old Testament prophets' words of condemnation and on the need for
repentance are set by their vision of the reign of God. Jesus's definition of his
ministry offers insights into authentic Christianity as he announces God's
Spirit upon him "to bring good news to the poor . . . to proclaim release to

---

1   Leonard Swidler, "Understanding Dialogue," in *Interfaith Dialogue at the Grass Roots* (Phil-
     adelphia: Ecumenical Press, 2008), 9–24.

the captives and recovery of sight to the blind, to let the oppressed go free, to proclaim the year of the Lord's favor."[2]

> *Every outer evil inevitably attracts from our own depths parts of ourselves that resemble it. To engage evil is therefore a spiritual act, because it will require of us the rare courage to face our own most ancient and intractable evils within.*
> —Walter Wink, *Jesus and Nonviolence: A Third Way*

That vision Jesus embodied in a transformative and transforming way defines Christianity as an agent of love and an agent against racism and all that divides people from one another and from God. Justice, informed by love, is key to understanding God's desire and purpose for human relationships and the communities and nation in which we live. *United Against Racism* is a call from churches to all Christians to embody an authentic Christianity; a Christianity of love, safety, openness, and freedom; a Christianity that prays, thinks, and takes action to end racism and all actions, behaviors, principles, practices, and policies that separate, divide, or harm human relationships. Authentic Christianity obligates Christians to acknowledge failures and to make restitution for wrongdoings in all areas of life. Equality of opportunity in employment, housing, and health care and the fair administration of the law are ethical indicators of the love, security, and freedom from the virus that contaminates relationships through double-minded words and actions. Justice demands respect, honor, and dignity for all persons and is inextricably tied to the authentic Christianity we affirm and promote for all people: black Americans, immigrant Americans, Latino/as, Asians, Native Americans, and white Americans. This study focuses on the black American experience because of its long and painful history, the breadth of oppression, and the ongoing battle for civil rights and social justice.

---

2   Luke 4:18–19.

*For the necessary transformation of our structures, racial eth-
nic people and their efforts must be seen as critically important
by the entire church. We must offer access and options for full
participation and representation to all people throughout the life
of the church, especially in its institutional structure. Positions of
leadership, authority, responsibility, decision and policy-making
and implementation should be entrusted to African Americans,
Asian Pacific Americans, Hispanics and Latin Americans and
Indigenous People. Racial ethnic executives must be treated as
professional peers by their white colleagues.*
—National Council of Churches statement

We believe God calls each person to join the holy work of claiming authentic Christianity today. This includes work to end racism in
all its forms. Such work begins by entering into conversations around
racial truth-telling, racial justice, repentance, reparation, forgiveness,
and, ultimately, transformation. Recognizing the image of God in every
person, let us work together for systemic change, seeking expressions of
God's love through full racial equality in all parts of our society.

The Christian's task is "to see what God is doing and join in," former
Archbishop of Canterbury Rowan Williams frequently said.[3] Let us all
join this holy and complicated, delicate, and difficult godly work for
racial justice in our society.

In Jesus Christ, all people of whatever race, caste, or ethnic descent
are reconciled to God and to each other. Racism as an ideology and
discrimination as a practice are a betrayal of the rich diversity of God's
design for the world and violate the dignity of human personality.
All forms of racism—whether individual, collective, or systemic—
must be named sin and their theological justification heresy.[4]

3   Rowan Williams, Archbishop's Presidential Address, General Synod, York, July 14,
     2003.
4   Michael Kinnamon, ed., *The Ecumenical Movement: An Anthology of Key Tests and
     Voices*, 2nd ed. (Geneva: World Council of Churches, 2016), 208.

Racial conflict in society today is a matter of long histories, entrenched institutions, and systemic patterns of life that continue to hold people of color in bondage. Racial conflict threatens people of color's security. It denies their personal and social freedoms. It is a hindrance to love and an obstacle to participating in a beloved community. People need be able to speak of their experiences in safety without risking defensiveness or rejection. "If people feel their truth hasn't been heard," Coventry Cathedral's canon priest for Reconciliation Ministry, the Rev. Sarah Hill, warns, "their justice hasn't been served."[5] There needs to be space for lament over the racial pain, wounds, and evils of the past and the devastating repercussions that ripple forward into today's forms of racism.

> *In the "Dialogue of the Head" we mentally reach out to "the other" to learn from those who think differently from us. . . . In the "Dialogue of the Hands" we join together with others to work to make the world a better place in which we all must live together. . . . In the "Dialogue of the Heart" we open ourselves to receive the beauty of "the other."*
> —Leonard Swidler, *Interfaith Dialogue at the Grass Roots*

People of color tire of trying to explain their experience to those who question its validity. British journalist Reni Eddo-Lodge's book, *Why I'm No Longer Talking to White People about Race*, describes the difficulty—indeed, for her, the impossibility—of getting past white defensiveness and disconnection on racial issues. For Eddo-Lodge, as for many other people of color, retelling stories of oppression and acknowledging the pain of ongoing racial injustice is simply traumatic and futile.[6]

> *Racism—a mix of power, privilege, and prejudice—is sin, a violation of God's intention for humanity. The resulting racial,*

---

5   Sarah Hills, luncheon remarks given at Virginia Theological Seminary, April 4, 2017.
6   Reni Eddo-Lodge, *Why I'm No Longer Talking to White People about Race* (London: Bloomsbury Circus, 2017).

ethnic, or cultural barriers deny the truth that all people are
God's creatures and, therefore, persons of dignity. Racism frac-
tures and fragments both church and society.
—Evangelical Lutheran Church in America statement

Many people of color are sick of defending a reality they cannot escape
but feel others cannot or will not see. That reality includes literally fearing
for their safety on the streets of American cities. As lawyer Bryan Stevenson relates, "People of color in the United States, particularly young black
men, are burdened with a presumption of guilt and dangerousness."[7] The
Rev. Kenneth James gives a powerful voice to outrage on behalf of young
black men who are silenced and murdered on our city streets. He argues
that the plight of black Americans in our society today is nothing less than a
form of genocide that must be stopped now.[8] Authentic Christianity offers
safety and security in a world of crippling ambivalence and duplicitous
actions. The criminal justice system in America is rife with racial inequity.
People of color see daily examples of racially based structural inequalities in
employment and economic opportunity, in housing and medical care,
in politics and voting districts, and in schools, and many are angry and
frustrated that whites in general either do not acknowledge or minimize
these inequalities. Authentic Christianity demands equal application of the
law and promotes equal treatment of everyone under the law.

In conversations about racial diversity, many white people fear confrontation. They fear being accused of insensitivity. They fear giving
offense. They fear being blamed for a history that they cannot change.
They fear the threat to a system of white privilege that they benefit
from and do not know how to break. Many white people want to be

---

7   Bryan Stevenson, forward to *America's Original Sin: Racism, White Privilege, and the*
     Bridge to a New America, by Jim Wallis (Grand Rapids, MI: Brazos, 2016), xii.
8   Kenneth Q. James, "The Voices of Too Many People Are Silenced," in *Thinking Theo-*
     logically about Mass Incarceration, ed. Antonios Kireopoulos, Mitzi J. Budde, and
     Matthew D. Lundberg (Mahwah, NJ: Paulist, 2017), 293–303; Kenneth Q. James,
     "On Violence and Genocide" (unpublished paper presented to the National Council
     of Churches Faith and Order Convening Table's Violence in an Age of Genocide
     Study Group, May 12, 2017).

seen as good and tolerant people and fear being accused of being big-
ots. When white supremacists and Ku Klux Klan members from thirty-
five states gathered in Charlottesville, Virginia, for a "Unite the Right"
rally on August 12, 2017, many white people were shocked that such
a march could take place today. Many people of color, however, were
not surprised that such a march was happening. In a dialogue between
white Episcopal priest Cayce Ramey and black priest Jabriel Ballentine
on the podcast *Racial Heresy*, Fr. Ramey challenges whites to confront
and repent the depth of the sin of racism and to acknowledge and confront what they do not want to see.[9]

> *No matter where you go as a white person in American society,*
> *no matter where you live, no matter who your friends and allies*
> *are, and no matter what you do to help overcome racism, you*
> *can never escape white privilege in America if you are white. I*
> *benefit from white privilege (and male privilege as well) every*
> *single day, and I don't have any more say in that than black men*
> *and women who experience the opposite.*
> —Jim Wallis, *America's Original Sin*

In his award-winning book, *America's Original Sin: Racism, White Privilege, and the Bridge to a New America*, Jim Wallis explains to white Americans the ways in which they all benefit from white privilege. He calls
upon white people to repent of white racism, to change their behaviors,
and to let go of their defensiveness. "Only by morally dying to our false
identity as white people—an identity created for violent, oppressive
profit—can we come alive to our true identity as human beings," Wallis
argues.[10] Calling for "reimagining whiteness," columnist Courtney Martin challenges "white anti-racist Americans to step forward and declare the

---

9   Fr. Jabriel Ballentine and Fr. Cayce Ramey, "Excommunicating White
     Supremacy—Redeeming the Church," *Racial Heresy* podcast, August 23, 2017,
     https://www.blubrry.com/racial_heresy/.
10   Wallis, *America's Original Sin*, 80.

dismantling of white supremacy a personal priority."[11] White Americans need to acknowledge the harm that has been inflicted upon people of color in the past and the ongoing experiences of exclusion and discrimination that they continue to experience today. Racism, white supremacy, and white privilege are hazards to authentic Christianity, a religion that claims that "perfect love casts out fear."[12]

There are some meaningful and relevant steps people can take to embody an inclusive, beloved community and the practices of authentic Christianity. The first step is to pray. According to a 2014 Pew Research Center survey, more than half of Americans (55 percent) indicated that they pray every day.

Much of the content of this book affirms our belief in prayer. The efficacy of prayer is not in the words humans express but in the God who hears and responds. Praying for God's will to become reality reframes the supplicant's understanding of what is right and just. Prayer is a privileged conversation with the God who, according to the Psalmist, will be a refuge and strength.[13] When Christians pray, they obligate themselves to join in the work of God and to follow the example and ways of Jesus Christ. The practice of praying for God's reign to come and God's will to be done is activity that helps persons become authentically Christian. Prayer aligns one's intentions to the will of God rather than sponsoring a one-way communication to inform God all about one's desires. The Omniscient God is aware.

A second action that can move people toward an inclusive, beloved community involves the work of building trust. While the instinctual drive toward self-preservation may initially direct people to fear, exclude, isolate, or segregate from others, we are inherently interconnected, and trust is essential for building and enhancing human relations. According to the 2012 "Portraits of American Life Study," large percentages of

---

11   Courtney E. Murray, "A New Narrative of Whiteness Is Unfolding," *On Being* (blog), with Krista Tippett, September 7, 2017, https://onbeing.org/blog/courtney -martin-a-new-narrative-of-whiteness-is-unfolding/.

12   1 John 4:18.

13   Ps. 46:1.

Americans completely or somewhat trust their neighbor (74 percent) or members of their congregation or parish (85 percent). How might we build upon these dispositions in our relating to one another across races and ethnic groups to express and embody authentic Christianity?

Just as trust is essential for building positive interpersonal and group relations, credibility is a necessary feature of trust. Across our nation, a common perception is that the trust gap between whites and people of color is widening rather than narrowing. While trust is too often taken for granted, skepticism about the "other" is growing. Stephen M. R. Covey and Rebecca R. Merrill (2014) suggest four components for establishing credibility: integrity, intent, capabilities, and results.[14] Integrity is also made up of four qualities: *honesty* refers to telling the truth, *congruence* involves alleviating any distance between what one says and what one does, *humility* expresses greater concern for *what is* right than concern for *being* right, and *courage* refers to a resolve to take the right action.[15]

Prayer and trust building can help to reclaim an authentic Christianity that seeks love over fear. We need humility and courage to name the problem and acknowledge the damage, pain, wounds, and hurtful legacy of the past and the power the past continues to inflict. "Hate left unchecked tends to escalate."[16] As individuals, we need to reach out to one another, to allow others to speak the truth of their experiences without defensiveness or rejection, to listen deeply to one another's perspectives, and to have the courage to speak our truth.

There is no fear in love, but perfect love casts our fear, for fear has to do with punishment, and whoever fears has not reached perfection in love.[17]

---

14   Stephen M. R. Covey and Rebecca R. Merrill, *The Speed of Trust: The One Thing That Changes Everything* (New York: Free Press, 2014), 43–58.

15   Covey and Merrill, 59–72.

16   Tom Perriello, "Virginia Needs a Truth and Reconciliation Commission on Race," *Washington Post*, September 6, 2017, https://www.washingtonpost.com/opinions/virginia-needs-a-truth-and-reconciliation-commission-on-race/2017/09/06/8f1a5bde-8e6d-11e7-8df5-c2e5cf46c1e2_story.html?utm_term=.229fee316926.

17   1 John 4:18.

Joseph V. Crockett, former associate general secretary at the National Council of Churches, asks, How do people who see things differently come to see them that way?[18] This question may help persons with differing views on racism come to understand the experiences behind their opinions. In so doing, it may help us overcome the limits of our understanding of another's experience and listen to one another's stories, the laments and the celebrations, with the ears and heart of Christ. Through Jesus Christ, we can know the truth and be set free by it.[19] In Christ, we can have the courage to hear and encounter one another's truth, to pray together, think about critical concerns, and act in ways that express and embody authentic Christianity.

A PRAYER FOR UNHEARING, UNLEARNING, AND UNWOUNDING

CHRISTIAN IOSSO
PRESBYTERIAN CHURCH (USA)

Indwelling God,

You speak to us all through the great pattern of a life bravely lived and given for others, a descent into loss and death, and an ascent into resurrection life. Every act of moral heroism responds to Your voice within us and confirms that paradoxical truth that "whoever would save his or her life must lose it." The story of Jesus breaks through all the monologues of power and connects us with the fire-edge of prophecy that threatens all injustice. The vision of a kingdom or reign of healing, freedom, and abundance calls us to strive for a whole creation redeemed and at peace. Let us keep our hands to the Gospel plow and never lose heart.

O God, we know Your call is to all people, but racism seems to derail our dreams of progress. We are seen differently and we see differently; we carry different burdens of awareness and history. We may value deeply

---

18   A question posed by Ray Dalio in *Principles*, audiobook, September 19, 2017.
19   John 8:32.

our cultures and traditions, yet we hear Your words through the prophet Amos: "Are you not like the Ethiopians to me, O people of Israel? Did I not bring up Israel from . . . Egypt, and the Philistines from Caphtor and the Syrians from Kir?"[20] You are a universal God who cares for all people; may we unhear the claims that any of us are uniquely deserving. May we cross lines and take stands that reflect Your sovereign love for "the least of these."

Living God, You warn us that You shake nations and thrones, and You speak to us in the voices of those who suffer for righteousness' sake: under terrifying bombs, in overcrowded prisons, on tear gas-engulfed streets, in dangerous and underpaid work, and at government and business posts when the demand comes to serve the rich and abandon the poor. Then we know there is an age-old struggle reflected in our color-coded caste and class system. To undo the structures and spectacles of domination means unlearning the habits and assumptions of privilege. This is harder than simply adopting new positions from someone else. Give those of us who have much of the world's favor both the courage to confess and the tenacity to remake the markets and polities that perpetuate inequality.

God of incarnation, let us come to see Your face in those of all others around us. As we rejoice in the bodies we have been given, let us celebrate the infinite diversity of human feature and form. When we behold each other in love, we know that all possess a beauty that is partly inward. Racism is a lens of fear and falsehood that distorts and blinds and helps the forces and people who wound others. What may have been a speck of disrespect has become over generations a log of latent hatred and reflexive resentment. Along with the repairs and reparations necessary for reconciliation, help us walk together to the places of unwounding, where God's Spirit heals and trust can be reborn. Let none claim to be totally whole, for the evil of racism leaves subtle scars. But let us know more of You, God, and Your colors of water and air, light and darkness, through which Your glory shines.

In the name of the One who still comes to save, Amen.

---

20   Amos 9:7.

PRAYER FOR PEACE THAT DISRUPTS US

APOSTLE JANNÉ C. GROVER
COMMUNITY OF CHRIST

God of Shalom,

Yours is the peace we proclaim, the peace we long for, and the peace that is realized when justice is our common purpose through Christ. The peace for which we strive is your kingdom, the kingdom that was present in Jesus. It is an upside-down kingdom where servanthood replaces political posturing, where "Us" and "Them" become "We," where human worth IS, and where creation is liberated from human greed.

We confess our complacency and complicity that keep true and lasting peace in fragile infancy at best. Forgive our resistance to confronting assumptions, biases, and prejudices that perpetuate racism and systems of injustice.

We know that if we proclaim the peace of Jesus Christ, then we must challenge the kingdoms of this world that promote fear, division, greed, violence, and needless suffering. Even as we pray for peace, we confess our unwillingness to courageously challenge cultural, political, and religious trends that are contrary to your reconciling and restoring purposes. Help us realize the transforming power of your shalom *if* we seek it with the intention of looking deeply into who we are and allow it to shape who we are called to be.

Disrupt our comfortable sense of "us-ness." Grant us the courage to open the borders of our hearts and welcome the "other" and recognize Christ in the faces of all your beloved children. Help us walk through this world awakened to what it means to belong to each other . . . to belong to your kingdom of shalom.

May our prayers for peace disrupt our status quo and lead us into actions of reconciliation, restoration, and justice for the sake of all the world you so dearly love.

We pray in the name of Jesus Christ, who is our peace. Amen.

PRAYER FOR NEW POSSIBILITIES

REV. JANET L. WOLF, DIRECTOR
ALEX HALEY FARM AND NONVIOLENT ORGANIZING
CHILDREN'S DEFENSE FUND

Gracious, awesome, and life-giving God,
we just come to say thank you.
Thank you for bringing us this far on the journey.
Thank you for glimmers of your glory and the power of your presence.
Thank you for the wideness of your mercy and the enoughness of your
grace.

We pray, O God, that you will forgive us,
for we know we have fallen short, each and every one of us.
We have settled into a comfortable compromise with the status quo.
We have been silent when you called us to speak.
We have domesticated your calls for deliverance, sitting on the side-
lines when you asked us to join you in the streets.
We are complicit with systems and structures that destroy, deny, dis-
miss, and belittle our sisters and brothers.
We have bowed down to the powers of death.

Forgive us, we pray, and by the power of your Holy Spirit, create in us
new possibilities for life.
Grant unto us the creative courage and holy boldness to live as your
people, to love in your name,
to confront and dismantle white supremacy and oppression in all its
forms,
to create a world in which all people have a right to the tree of life.

Heal our land.
Renew our vision.

Revive our spirits.
Restore unto us the joy of thy salvation.

Make us new, Creator God.
Challenge our complacency.
Disturb our apathy.
Set us on fire with a holy passion for justice and a fierce and never-ending love for all your creation.
In your holy name we pray. Amen.

A MILLENNIAL LAMENT

TANYA Y. BOUCICAUT
VIRGINIA COMMONWEALTH UNIVERSITY

O God,
We millennials are angry, hurt, and in dismay.
We've discovered that generations before us lied about this land being the home of the free and land of the brave.
They told us we lived in a "post" society:
    postracist
    postsexist
    postclassist
Yet many refuse to see our young black bodies slain by the police.
Yet many refuse to see our schools' funding are still segregated.
We are. Yet we are ignored and silenced by the Church.

What is jarring to our souls is this intergenerational divide of racism.
It didn't start with us. Where did it come from?
How did it seep in our collective consciousness?
A legacy and culture of hate. We get it.
We wonder, How do we fix a broken system we didn't create?
And it still hurts . . .

The fragility of our humanity causes us to mourn as products of a racist society we didn't architect.

But today is a new day. A day where we hold everyone accountable. We're calling everyone to the carpet.

But thank You, O God; the winds are changing . . .
You're prophesizing to a different generation.
Like in Acts, we're prophesizing and seeing visions . . .

Our dreams are different. Our goals are different. Our visions are different.

Visions of a better tomorrow.
Visions of racial equity.
We have that #blackgirlmagic and #blackboyjoy

Lord, we millennials feel the winds are changing . . .

Thanks to be You, O Lord, the God of our ancestors and older generations, we are recognizing the winds changing.

IN THE MIDST OF DISTRESS

DONALD H. ASHMALL
INTERNATIONAL COUNCIL OF COMMUNITY CHURCHES

God of our past, our present, and our future, Ruler of all that has been, is, and ever shall be: we worship You as our Creator, our Redeemer, and our Companion in time and beyond.

We come to You now confessing that our prideful pretensions have been beaten down and crushed. Our expectations have been shattered into cutting shards that cause our spirits to bleed. Our plans have come to naught, and our expectations have been made a mockery. Yet we dare to proclaim that our hope is not in vain. Though we may be enduring the worst of days, we live in faithful expectation of the best of days yet to come. Though we are forced to endure a long night of sorrow and grief, we know that joy will come in the morning. That which is hateful and hate filled will one day give way to the influence of Your compassionate Spirit, and when that day comes that all of creation is weighed in the balance scales, love will triumph.

So we worship You in confidence, knowing that in the midst of our struggles, Your presence will never leave or forsake us. There truly is a balm in the Gilead of our souls, and whatever the ails of our spirits may be, by Your mercy, we will be healed.

However battered and bruised we may feel, and wounded though we may be, send us forth this day to ministries of mercy. Aid us as we seek to help the helpless. Cause us to love even the unlovely. Free us to unbind those held captive. Give us the insight to proclaim and to live justice, even in a world that denies it to so many. Help us persist in service to all Your people, revealing to us in our labors that peace that passes all understanding, even as we celebrate Your coming victory.

We pray it in the name of the risen and living Christ.

Amen.

Think about It. Talk about It.

What truth-telling about race are you longing to speak? To hear from others?

What fears do you have around conversations about race, and how might you overcome them?

Engage

Discuss your responses to the following questions:

1. What race/ethnicity do you consider yourself to be?

2. Are there any members of other races/ethnicities living in *your* neighborhood now (personal/church)?
   a. Yes   b. No   c. Don't know   d. Pass

3. Do you feel in any way discriminated against where you work, worship, or live because of your race/ethnicity?
   a. Yes   b. No   c. Don't know   d. Pass

If yes, talk about the discrimination you experience.

Respond to the next two questions using a scale of 0 to 6, with 0 representing "Not at all" and 6 representing "Completely."

4. How much do you find that being [respondent's race] influences or guides how you behave? Where you live?
   Not at all—0   1   2   3   4   5   6—Completely

5. How much do you think people in the US respect [respondent's race/ethnicity]?
   Not at all—0   1   2   3   4   5   6—Completely

Go Deeper. Read More.
DiAngelo, Robin. *What Does It Mean to Be White? Developing White Racial Literacy.* New York: Peter Lang, 2012.
Perkinson, James. *White Theology: Outing Supremacy in Modernity (Black Religion/Womanist Thought/Social Justice).* New York: Palgrave Macmillan, 2004.

WHEN YOUR JUSTICE DOESN'T LOOK OR FEEL LIKE MY JUSTICE

The righteous know the rights of the poor;
the wicked have no such understanding.

—Proverbs 29:7

Key Terms

JUSTICE, a term at the heart of the Judeo-Christian prophetic tradition, rejects any sense of salvation that is indifferent to the needs and conditions of humankind. While divine love pushes humanity beyond its temporal concerns, divine love does not exist without justice.

RESTORATIVE JUSTICE seeks to restore dignity to both victim and perpetrator, not just to overcome the harm done, but also to offer mediation and the opportunity for truth-telling for the sake of reconciliation.

RETRIBUTIVE JUSTICE tries to rebalance the injury done to society by addressing whatever wrongdoing has occurred.

TRANSFORMATIVE JUSTICE includes restorative justice but moves beyond it to transform the societal structures that allowed the injustice to occur in the first place.

TRANSITIONAL JUSTICE means working to stabilize a situation and set up structures to pursue justice.

How do we work together to create a more just society? What does justice look like? What kind of justice do we seek?

The courtroom of popular opinion on social media is sometimes quick to act without due process and to judge on the basis of little, or even false, evidence. Contradictory accounts of the same incident are told from

different political perspectives for various ulterior motives. Yet network-
ing sometimes works effectively in situations of injustice that need a
unified voice of protest. When six police officers were exonerated in
Baltimore after Freddie Gray, a black man, died of a spinal injury in
their custody in 2015, the public forum cried out for justice. In the
absence of a just verdict in the legal system, the only justice available
may be *justice* mediated through social media: naming and shaming
through public outcry.

Alas for you who desire the day of the Lord!
   Why do you want the day of the Lord?
It is darkness, not light;
   as if someone fled from a lion,
   and was met by a bear;
or went into the house and rested a hand against the wall,
   and was bitten by a snake.[1]

An inclusive, beloved community living under the banner of Christianity sets forth a set of habits and practices that fosters well-being in a
world of harm and danger. In the legal system in the United States, justice is generally transitional and/or retributive. *Transitional justice* means
working to stabilize a situation and set up structures to pursue justice:
stopping violence, helping victims cope, reestablishing peace, and creating structures for accountability (e.g., hearings, trials). For example, in
the immediate aftermath of a police shooting of an unarmed black man,
transitional justice would put the police officer on leave and set up a
process of gathering witness information and responding to community
questions and protests.

Retributive justice tries to rebalance the injury done to society by
addressing whatever wrongdoing has occurred. Its focus is identifying
and punishing the perpetrator in proportion to what was done. For
example, retributive justice would call for the arrest and conviction of a

---

1   Amos 5:18–19.

police officer who shot an unarmed black motorist when the legal process has determined the action unjustified.

*[Justice as fairness consists of] two rather different principles: the
first requires equality in the assignment of basic rights and duties,
while the second holds that social and economic inequalities . . . are
just only if they result in compensating benefits for everyone, and
in particular for the least advantaged members of society.*
                                    —John Rawls, *Theory of Justice*

Transitional justice and retributive justice are integral to a demo-
cratic society. As Christians, however, we seek justice as an expression
of divine love and a witness to the authentic life that Jesus lived. It
is a justice that establishes or reestablishes right relationships between
individuals and communities and empowers people with the agency to
return to the community. *Restorative justice* seeks to restore dignity
to both victim and perpetrator, not just to overcome the harm done,
but also to offer mediation and the opportunity for truth-telling for the
sake of reconciliation. Authentic Christianity requires acknowledgment
and appropriate restitution for wrongdoings. So in the police shooting scenario, restorative justice would establish conversations between
a police force and a predominantly minority community, working to
improve relations and trust on both sides. Through restorative justice, a
police officer whose legal innocence has been upheld might yet be able
to acknowledge having done something morally and spiritually wrong.

Transformative justice includes restorative justice but moves beyond it
to transform the societal structures that allowed the injustice to occur in
the first place. Theologically it looks like Isaiah 58:6: "to loose the bonds
of injustice, to undo the thongs of the yoke, to let the oppressed go free,
and to break every yoke." In the same example of the police shooting
of an unarmed black man, transformative justice would impel systemic
changes to the criminal justice system in this country.

Authentic Christianity is concerned with all of these forms of justice—
transitional, retributive, restorative, and *transformative*—while recognizing

that each is an approximation but not a substitute for self-sacrificing love. Christians who strive to live authentically work to establish standards and structures of justice. They are more concerned with a perpetrator's acknowledgement of wrongdoing and his or her turning to a new way of being and relating to others than they are with "punishing" a person for wrongful acts. Authentic Christianity recognizes that punishment alone is not redemptive. Societal change necessitates that Christians stand and work shoulder to shoulder with every other citizen of the world to repair its brokenness and to make it more loving and just. True followers of Jesus obligate themselves to hold up the hope that honesty will prevail over hypocrisy and that truth has roots in responsible action and mutual respect.

Becoming aware of God's concern for the world helps us discern the need for justice. Jesus summed up the law for followers who would strive to live authentically in terms of relationships: "You shall love the Lord your God with all your heart, and with all your soul, and with all your strength, and with all your mind; and your neighbor as yourself."[2] And without leaving room for error, Jesus, according to Luke, makes clear who is one's neighbor: the outcast, the marginalized, the oppressed—those in need. Leonardo Boff wrote, "Jesus' whole preaching may be seen as an effort to awaken the strength of these community aspects. In the horizontal dimension Jesus called human beings to mutual respect, generosity, a communion of sisters and brothers, and simplicity in relationships. Vertically, he sought to open the human being to a sincere filial relationship with God, to the artlessness of simple prayer, and to generous love for God."[3]

According to the 2010 Baylor Religions Survey, people perceive a difference between God's concern for the world's well-being and God's involvement to bring it about. While 86 percent "strongly agree" or "agree" that God is concerned with the well-being of the world, just over half (51 percent) perceive that God is directly involved. For some of those

2   Luke 10:27.
3   Leonardo Boff, *Ecclesiogenesis: The Base Communities Reinvent the Church* (Maryknoll, NY: Orbis Books, 1986), 7.

who believe that God is not directly involved (49 percent) in the world's affairs, they might also think that God has a role for them. They might be seeking ways to become a Good Samaritan, to extend God's heart and to be God's hands in ways that promote inclusivity, love, security, openness, and freedom to work against racism, bigotry, and discrimination.

The biblical teachings are rich with suggestions for those who want to be involved in building an inclusive, beloved community as a worthy expression of an authentic Christianity. Here are some ideas from Paul's letter to the community of Jesus's followers in Rome:

Let love be genuine; hate what is evil, hold fast to what is good;[4]
love one another with mutual affection;
outdo one another in showing honor.[5]
Contribute to the needs of the saints;
extend hospitality to strangers.[6]
Live in harmony with one another.[7]
Do not repay anyone evil for evil, but take thought for what is noble in the
sight of all.[8]

PRAYER OF CONFESSION

JIM WINKLER
NATIONAL COUNCIL OF CHURCHES

Dear God,

We confess to you once again that we have not loved you with our whole hearts nor with all our minds. Neither have we loved our neighbors as much as we love ourselves and those who look like us.

---

4   Rom. 12:9.
5   Rom. 12:10.
6   Rom. 12:13.
7   Rom. 12:16.
8   Rom. 12:17.

Rather, we have divided ourselves based on false distinctions of skin color and systematized those differences to permit lighter-hued peoples to exploit those with a darker hue. This is sin. We know that with your forgiveness comes the responsibility to forego privileges based on lies, theft, cruelty, murder, and slavery.

Give to those who benefit from systemic sin the strength and resolve to make atonement, to rectify injustice, and to walk humbly alongside you.

Release the privileged from the imprisonment of false stereotypes. Grant them vision to see their sisters and brothers as your children and not as "others."

Give to those who benefit from white privilege the courage to renounce their entitlement and to accept that God's justice requires not only societal change but alterations in the lives of each person.

Make us instruments of truth and transformation.

It is to you we turn with gratitude. It is to you we turn for renewal. It is to you we turn for restoration.

Lead us to the hour when we will end racism and heal the nation.

May you, O God, our God, bless the houses of worship of our land that they work together to build the beloved community.

Amen.

LORD, WE'RE WEARY

REV. JEFFERY L. TRIBBLE SR., PHD
SOUTH ATLANTIC EPISCOPAL DISTRICT DIRECTOR
OF CONTINUING EDUCATION
AFRICAN METHODIST EPISCOPAL ZION CHURCH

I confess a weariness with the oppressive experience of racism that I have known as a black person in America—the constant struggle of persons of color just to "be" and to become all that the Creator intends for every child of God. I'm weary of the hostility endured just for "being black" in so many spaces and places—for "being black" while driving and confronted with hostile police officers, for "being black" while laboring in hostile predominantly white institutions, even for "being black" and murdered while in a prayer meeting in Charleston, South Carolina.

More than ever, we need what Dr. King called the "strength to love." In this present "age of Trump," my mind is drawn to reflect this verse: "Let love be genuine; hate what is evil, hold fast to that which is good."[9] But if love would be strong and genuine, we must be discerning about that which is truly evil and that which is good.

I pray that you would teach the body of Christ to truly hate the evil of racism and white supremacy. This evil is intertwined with wealth and privilege built on the backs of so many of *my* people whose lives are structured by systems of oppression that severely limit our life chances and life choices: family systems, educational systems, social service systems, political and economic systems, criminal justice systems, and even religious systems.

At the same time, I pray that we "hold fast to that which is good"— our God-given capacity to faithfully reflect the image of God. Help us "to not be overcome with evil, but to overcome evil with good."[10] I pray for trustworthy white-identifying allies in this work of justice and righteousness—those who would stay the course of ending racism.

A PAN-AFRICAN CHRISTIAN PRAYER THAT CALLS FOR LOVE, JUSTICE, AND MERCY

REV. DR. ANGELIQUE WALKER-SMITH
NATIONAL BAPTIST CONVENTION

CALL TO PRAYER: Our God loves us more than we can possibly imagine. We give thanks to God that God's imagination and creation

---

9   Rom. 12:9.
10   Rom. 12:21.

includes all people and not just certain people who conform to our limited individual and collective lens of bias and parochialism.

PRAYERFUL AFFIRMATION: Let us rejoice in the ways God has made this possible!

CALL TO PRAYER: Although the economy of wealth and white privilege was built on the sin of slave labor of Pan-African people and the creation of unjust laws that have denied Pan-African people a good education and equity in this economy, people of Africa and of African descent have resisted these injustices and not only have left a wise legacy but continue to do this. This despite lack of due recognition and appreciation in the dominant and privileged globalized Eurocentric culture.

PRAYERFUL AFFIRMATION: Yet we know that our God's love, justice, and mercy are intimately placed in the heart of God for all God's children!

CALL TO PRAYER: Although there are still unjust laws that codify institutional racism that contribute to the disproportionate economic and hunger disparities of people of Africa and African descent, laws have been reformed. Still, more legal and relational reforms are needed to more effectively reflect inclusive principles. Such can and must contribute to the vision of justice and mercy that moves us toward the more beloved community that the Rev. Dr. Martin Luther King Jr. and many others espoused.

PRAYERFUL AFFIRMATION: Our acceptance of God's present and eternal devotion to all of us should be demonstrated in a lifestyle that actively embraces the eternal principles of love, beauty, and shalom toward all people. May it be so.

CALL TO PRAYER: Philippians 4:8–9 invites us to live lives of faith that demonstrate that which is true, honorable, just, pure, lovely, gracious, excellent, and worthy of praise. We are invited to think about these things. We are reminded that what we have learned, received, heard, and seen about God, we are to do, and the God of peace will be with us.

PRAYERFUL AFFIRMATION: Our God's grace and faithfulness is sufficient and empowers us to decry racial hatred and racist laws and practices.

CALL TO PRAYER: One of the favorite hymns in black American churches, "We've Come This Far by Faith," reminds us that there is a great legacy of people of faith who have resisted all forms of discrimination. May we remember that such resistance and faithfulness is still required.

PRAYERFUL AFFIRMATION: Our God's continual presence and power emboldens us to be faithful to the vision of the beloved community! Let us rejoice! May our hearts burn with passion for the calling for which God has set before us individually and collectively even as we serve our God and all of God's people and the rest of his divine and magnificent creation! Amen.

PRAYER OF PROTEST

W. DARIN MOORE, BISHOP
AFRICAN METHODIST EPISCOPAL ZION CHURCH

Our gracious, just, and loving God,

You sent Your prophet Isaiah and Your Son Jesus to us with the mission "to bring good news to the oppressed, to bind up the brokenhearted, to proclaim liberty to the captives, and release to the prisoners; to proclaim the year of the Lord's favor and the day of vengeance of our God; to comfort all who mourn."[11] We need this good news today for those who are oppressed and for those accountable for oppression, for those who are brokenhearted and for those responsible for brokenness, for those bound and for those who hold them in bondage, for those who mourn and for those who are the cause or source of grief. Forgive us if we are blind to the plight of those who cry out of their pain or if we fail to see the fear of those who live in daily despair because we do not acknowledge their concerns. The powerful and the powerless are equally fearful; deliver us from our fears. The

---

11   Isa. 61:1b–2.

mighty and the weak are equally apprehensive; save us from our narrow perspectives. Teach us to know and truly and fully acknowledge our brother and sister as our brother and sister, not as some "other" of whom we must be wary.

The prayerful protests of our brothers and sisters reach the heavens; we love and serve a God who answers prayer. So when the oppressed out of their grief pray, "Hear my cry, O God; listen to my prayer. From the end of the earth I call to you, when my heart is faint. Lead me to the rock that is higher than I,"[12] You, God, are listening. And when bullies and tyrants turn and pray in humility, "O Lord, my heart is not lifted up, my eyes are not raised too high; I do not occupy myself with things too great and too marvelous for me,"[13] those prayers reach Your heavenly throne also.

You alone, Yahweh, are our hope, our reason for confidence, and the source of our courage. You, Lord, are our light and salvation; whom shall we fear? You, God, are the strength of our lives; of whom shall we be afraid? We pray to be released of our fears from all forces of evil that separate us from others of Your children and pray for renewed trust and grace to trust You and Your promises more. Amen.

Heart for the City: The Sound of a Black Boy

Donté McCutchen

Kind spirit, God of the heavens and the Earth, I want to know, can you see what I see?

There are cities filled with mothers and fathers crying because their children are dying. Social status and class are keeping us separated and ignored. Our spirits are on life support, and people who don't look like me threaten to pull the plug. Help us, Creator, we need a family

---

12   Ps. 61:1–2.
13   Ps. 131:1.

reunion. Bring all who wear the badge of salvation together. We are brothers and sisters, and it will only be known by our love.

What would it look like if we really lived in community? I know you have the power to bring our hands together and cause a heavenly melody to be played by your children on every street in every neighborhood. I pray this prayer with my grandmother in my mind, and I remember her spirit. Give us a world filled with praying grandmothers. The God of Viola McCutchen, I call on you right now. Reconcile differences, and let us come to the table and dine together. Feed us, O God of Dr. Martin Luther King Jr. The world hungers for a plate of peace. What would it look like if we really lived in community? Feed us until our complexions no longer are an excuse for the destruction we cause.

I am black, Lord, but I am yours, and I need you to hear me. Do you hear the prayers of little black boys from the inner cities of America? Do you really know the number of hairs on my head even though it's coarse? I know you're real because you helped my ancestors. We need the help you gave before. We've been stuck in the mess of racism for far too long. The world needs a taste of you, Jesus.

My spirit echoes Psalm 13, verses 1 and 2: "How long, Lord? Will you forget me forever? How long will you hide your face from me? How long must I wrestle with my thoughts and day after day have sorrow in my heart? How long will my enemy triumph over me?"

Our hearts break because we've never been equal. Our heads ache because we can't understand.

What would it look like to be whole? I pray for the day of only "us" and not a "them." God of the angel armies, we need you to move through the land and purify intentions. We want to live, but some days it seems more promising to die. The ways of those who have deemed themselves superior have stolen our voices and paralyzed the language of the souls of our bodies. Our dance has slowed down, and our song has changed.

Restore to us the joy of our culture. Restore to us the faith of those who have gone on before us. Keep your victories on our minds. You've already won, so when it looks like defeat, we remember your ability.

Great king and awesome ruler, be our God. You are the God of cohesiveness. Teach us to work together. Teach us to love you so well that we love like you. You long to become the Lord of our lives, so show off like only you can; fix our land. You know what we would look like if we really lived in community. Help us see what you see.

PRAYER OF JUSTICE FOR RACIAL EQUALITY

SYLVESTER WILLIAMS SR., BISHOP
CHRISTIAN METHODIST EPISCOPAL CHURCH

Dear God,

Every morning you allow us to rise to the dawning beauty of a new day. We see the sun tiptoe across the horizon, dispelling the darkness of night. We witness the sun's rays that warm the earth or the cool breezes regulating the temperature of the day. Rain counters the drought and seasons come and go. We see beauty and harmony in your created universe; we sing, "O Lord my God, how great thou art." Yet in a world so beautiful and harmonious, we witness inequalities, injustices, oppression, and so on, largely resulting from racism, classism, sexism, and greed, to name a few. Hear us now, O God, we most humbly beseech you. Being aware of these issues, help us amend our actions that perpetuate entities and systems that foster these ills. But let justice roll down like waters, and righteousness like an everflowing stream. Deliver us from support, silence, complacency, or any action that doesn't hold us accountable. Help us have your will and spirit lest we become so absorbed in greed and personal agendas that we fail to recognize the "oneness" of your spirit and that "all men are created equal." Give us hearts that do not foster fault finding and blame but repentance and forgiveness. Bless us as the people who are called by your name to be catalysts for combatting all evils, but especially the many facets of racism that breed injustice, inequality, dehumanization, or anything that is antagonistic to your will. Give us Pentecostal experiences that encourage us not only to use all our gifts and resources but to be bold and courageous as we speak, challenge, and promote love, unity, and equality to address and end racism. In the name of Jesus, we pray. Amen.

PRAYER FOR NEW TOOLS

RANDY G. LITCHFIELD, PhD
METHODIST THEOLOGICAL SCHOOL

Justice-seeking God, we want to partner with you in the work of the Kin-dom.[14] Yet the tools we have are the ones that built and maintain the master's house of racism and white privilege. Sister Audre Lorde testified, "The master's tools will never dismantle the master's house."[15] The tools many of us have will not do. Help us lay aside the tools that

maintain our obliviousness to privilege,
    put people of color in the role of teaching about being white,
        create exit doors for us when things get uncomfortable,
            preserve our privilege by "including" others,
                obscure the role of our aggressions in pyramids of violence,
                relieve our feeling of guilt without demanding
                transformation.

Carpenter of Nazareth, make the handles of these tools too splintered to hold, too heavy to pick up, too broken to use. We repent of their use.

---

14   The term *Kin-dom* places more emphasis on our relationship with God and one another than the term *kingdom*, which implicitly, if not explicitly, connotes hierarchical relations and structures of dominance. See Ada María Isasi-Díaz, *En La Lucha* (Minneapolis, MN: Fortress, 2004), 4.

15   Audre Lorde, *Sister Outsider: Essays and Speeches* (Trumansburg, NY: Crossing Press, 1984), 112.

Redeeming God, grace us with tools that build your House, your Kin-dom, where all can dwell in peace with justice. Do not leave us empty handed. Help us pick up the tools that

weave our lives together in common cause,
    enable us to understand whiteness so we may be in deep dialogue,
        create courage and solidarity so that exit doors swing closed,
           empower everyone to participate in the ongoing process of
           place making,
              gauge our well-being by whether the lives of persons of
              color truly matter,
                transform the *guilt* of power into the *gift* of power that
                liberates.

Carpenter of Nazareth, make the handles of these tools supple to grasp, easy to carry, graceful to use. Let us learn the craft of these tools in the company of others. May we together not only dismantle the master's house of racism and white privilege but build places where life and your Spirit flourish as well. Amen.

AN IDEAL WHOSE TIME HAS COME

GEORGE E. BATTLE JR., BISHOP
SENIOR BISHOP
AFRICAN METHODIST EPISCOPAL ZION CHURCH

Then Peter began to speak to them: "I truly understand that God shows no partiality, but in every nation anyone who fears him and does what is right is acceptable to him."[16]

Lord, hear our prayer for the United States of America.

16   Acts 10:34.

A nation founded as an experiment in democracy, predicated on the equality of men and certain unalienable rights, struggled through blood, sweat, and tears to realize the vision enshrined in the Declaration of Independence, a grand ideal but constitutionally flawed from its very inception by the notion that some human beings were only three-fifths human. This ideological aberration sanctified the continuance of slavery and the dehumanization of the African in America. Still racism plagues the land as the country approaches its sestercentennial. The nation's predilection to show favor to some and disfavor to others has once again pushed the nation to the precipice of ruin.

We turn to you, our God, to inspire those of us who portend to be your ambassadors, to save our nation from the harrowing of racism and its consequences. We implore you, O Lord, to empower us to persuade a nation to live up to the ideal of its creed, for we believe that if the nation is faithful to the ideal of the equality of all people, the country will mirror your vision of the kingdom.

Thus may we speak truth to power by word and nonviolent civil protest. May our words and actions articulate the vision of "beloved community," a society that embraces inclusivity, diversity, civil rights, and the social equality of all of God's people, showing no partiality. It is an ideal whose time has come. If the grand experiment of democracy is to flourish, it will by honoring the mutuality of all people, whose right it is to fully participate in the opportunities and resources that our nation affords the few.

May our words and actions always be guided by love.

Amen!

Think about It. Talk about It.

Do you "strongly agree," "agree," "disagree," or "strongly disagree" that God is concerned with the well-being of the world? What informs your view?

Do you "strongly agree," "agree," "disagree," or "strongly disagree" that God is directly involved in the world's affairs? What informs your opinion?

How do your views and opinions move you to act?

What kinds of justice are you seeking in your life?

Why do you shy away from engagement with racial injustice? Why do you think others do?

How could you challenge racism in your context?

Engage

Discuss your responses to the following questions:

1. Form a group and develop a list of characteristics participants believe to be marks of authentic Christianity that can be assessed as expressions of an inclusive, beloved community. How might the characteristics and practices encourage dialogue among people of different races and be the start of shared ministry?

2. Hold a discussion about which type(s) of justice (transitional, retributive, restorative, or transformative) does the best job of addressing the concerns listed below?

   a. Diffusing anger
   b. Providing compensation
   c. Seeking justice
   d. Making amends
   e. Redistributing undeserved gains
   f. Reconciling divisions
   g. Bringing closure
   h. Repairing wrongs

Go Deeper. Read More.

Higginbotham, A. Leon, Jr. *Shades of Freedom: Racial Politics and Presumptions of the American Legal Process*. New York: Oxford University Press, 1996.

Unander, Dave. *Shattering the Myth of Race: Genetic Realities and Biblical Truths*. Valley Forge, PA: Judson Press, 2000.

TESTIMONIES OF FAITH

DR. REX M. ELLIS
ASSOCIATE DIRECTOR FOR CURATORIAL AFFAIRS
NATIONAL MUSEUM OF AFRICAN AMERICAN HISTORY AND CULTURE
(NMAAHC) AT THE SMITHSONIAN INSTITUTION

*Joshua said to them, "Pass on before the ark of the Lord your God
into the middle of the Jordan, and each of you take up a stone
on his shoulder, one for each of the tribes of the Israelites, so that
this may be a sign among you. When your children ask in time to
come, 'What do those stones mean to you?' then you shall tell them
that the waters of the Jordan were cut off in front of the ark of the
covenant of the Lord. When it crossed over the Jordan, the waters
of the Jordan were cut off. So these stones shall be to the Israelites a
memorial forever."*

—Joshua 4:5–7

Key Terms

KNIGHTS OF THE KU KLUX KLAN, also known as the KKK, was founded in 1866.
Initially, the KKK was a tool for white southern resistance against
Reconstruction policies aimed at implementing political and economic equality for blacks after the Civil War.[1] Today, the KKK is made
up of three movements—white supremacy, white nationalism, and
anti-immigration—that vigorously oppose racial diversity and an inclusive society.

---

1   From the History Channel, http://www.history.com.

The *NATIONAL MUSEUM OF AFRICAN AMERICAN HISTORY AND CULTURE* is the only national museum devoted exclusively to the documentation of African American life, history, and culture, established in 2003.[2]

PLESSY V. FERGUSON was a historic case argued before the US Supreme Court on April 13, 1896. Homer A. Plessy, a free-born resident of the state of Louisiana of mixed lineage, challenged the practice of racial segregation by a railroad company. John H. Ferguson, a Louisiana judge, ruled that the state of Louisiana could regulate railroad companies that only operated within the confines of the state. The Supreme Court upheld Judge Ferguson's ruling that the "separate but equal" provision of private services was constitutional.

Through Faith, a Museum Is Established

The history of the Smithsonian National Museum of African American History and Culture dates back to 1915, when black Civil War veteran soldiers met on the National Mall in Washington, DC, to celebrate the fiftieth anniversary of the end of the Civil War. Black soldiers who survived that war encamped on the National Mall—the center of democracy—to honor those living and dead who sacrificed so much as well as to commemorate the reunion of our nation.

This was an annual event that had taken place every year since the end of the war, but this was the first year that black troops were invited. Imagine with me—can you see it? The black war heroes looking around the mall, which looked quite different than it does now, but realizing even then that they were in the nation's backyard. And as they stood there, we wonder if they asked themselves whether what they fought for—liberty and justice for all—had any real, lasting impact and whether they were truly an acknowledged part of that memory.

By 1915, the US Supreme Court case of *Plessy v. Ferguson* had been decided, and the court ruled that "separate but equal" would become the law of the land. Segregation laws that discriminated against black

---

2   From the National Museum of African American History and Culture, http://www
.nmaahc.si.edu.

Americans spread across the nation. Persons of color were required to be separated from whites in railroad cars, buses, train depots, hotels, theaters, restaurants, barber shops, and other establishments.[3] This was also the year that a watershed moment in cinematic and cultural history took place with the release of a movie called *The Birth of a Nation*. It was an adaptation of a novel written by Thomas Dixon Jr., who was a lawyer, actor, lecturer, North Carolina state legislator, and a southern Baptist minister. The novel follows two white families—one from the North and the other from the South—who both find themselves in South Carolina during the Reconstruction era, a period from roughly 1865 to 1877, when the states that were formerly part of the Confederacy were brought back into the United States. Although these two families fought on separate sides, they now are united in their opposition to newly freed slaves.

The film offers gross misrepresentations of blacks, including caricatures of black people. There are images of uncivilized black legislators and lustful and sexually violent black men—whose only objective in life is to prey on unwilling white women—and most black characters are played by white actors in blackface. Blacks are represented as the enemy, and the Ku Klux Klan are portrayed as the saviors as they forcefully fight against South Carolina's black population and threaten, attack, beat, and victimize them until they are convinced that their best course of action is to give up their right to vote and stay home. The film was a triumph for those sympathetic to the Confederacy and white supremacy and a nightmare to newly freed blacks—all four million of them.

So the same year black veterans were in town to commemorate the success of the Civil War and the abolition of slavery, a backlash that stood against the very freedom they had fought for had already begun. By 1916, the Committee of Colored Citizens launched a campaign to

---

3   Elizabeth Abel, *Signs of the Times: The Visual Politics of Jim Crow* (Berkeley: University of California Press, 2010); Michael J. Klarman, "The Progressive Era," in *From Jim Crow to Civil Rights: The Supreme Court and the Struggle for Racial Equality* (New York: Oxford University Press, 2004), 61–97; http://www.history.com/topics/black-history/black-history-milestones.

honor the contributions of black American soldiers. Perhaps it was the reality of their environment that convinced them they needed to find a way to honor the sacrifices of those who had fought and those who had died so that their progeny would have a true right to the "tree of life" as was part of democracy's promise. Perhaps they just opened their eyes and looked around them.

Faith's Journey

Faith was in short supply in the slave ships engorged with enslaved Africans. But faith through prayer started on the shores of Africa,[4] from Senegal in the west, and spread to Angola in the east. The prayers were to Ogun and Orishala in languages long forgotten, prayers that convinced mothers losing children and fathers separated from their families that trouble wouldn't last forever. It was faith that was kindled even aboard those slave ships, where horror became the norm and man's inhumanity to man would test captives in unimaginable ways.

Thinking about race in America, it causes one to ponder, How do you buttress the belief that all hope is not lost, that there is a way? How do you even keep "mustard-seed faith" when faced with a hopeless situation?

A relevant religious faith is practical. It is called into service and applied to the historical situation and contextual experiences of its followers.[5] This was the faith that provided comfort as newly arrived Africans felt the full effect of being "strangers in a strange land," surrounded by the unfamiliar and dependent on men and women who were convinced they were less than human. It was faith that searched for God in the land of the godless. It was faith that looked for hope in the presence of hopelessness. It was faith that took them through a revolution, a Civil

---

4 Two detailed accounts of the remaking of religion by enslaved Africans in the colonies are presented in Eugene D. Genovese, *Roll, Jordan, Roll: The World the Slaves Made* (New York: Vintage Books, 1972); Albert J. Raboteau, *Slave Religion, the "Invisible Institution" in the Antebellum South*, rev. ed. (New York: Oxford University Press, 2004).

5 Genovese, *Roll, Jordan, Roll*; Raboteau, *Slave Religion*.

War, to freedom on paper and hope beyond freedom's first blush. It was faith that found evidence every day that convinced them of the belief that, although their heads were bowed, they would not remain bent. It was faith that reminded them that like Job, though they might be slayed, their trust remained in God.[6] It was faith that found comfort in a man called Jesus, who knew of suffering; knew of distress; knew of pain; knew of hate; knew what it meant to be spat on, humiliated, scourged, whipped, and beaten. This messiah reminded them of a father who loved them despite what the world had done and continued to do.

Returning to the National Museum of African American History and Culture, this is what you will find, floor after floor, exhibit after exhibit, in paintings, artifacts, and text panels around corners and on the ceilings.

Faith can also be found at the National Museum of African American History and Culture. As you gaze upon the museum displays, sometimes faith will be obvious; sometimes it will not. Sometimes you will have to search for it in the stories as they are narrated through the signs. Sometimes faith will be difficult to find: in the midst of the horrors of war, in the degradation of lynching, in the failures of Reconstruction, in a little boy's horrible death at the hands of men who never really knew him . . . or in a contemporary environment that looks too much like the history we thought had died a natural death.

You will find that faith in sports, in the military, and in visual arts; you will find it in the spaces and places we lived around the nation. You'll find it where we made a way out of no way. You'll find it in music and the performing arts—in all the corners of our culture, you will find that faith that survived the torture, the emasculation, the lynching, the inhumanity, and the challenges we continue to face.

That is the faith you will see in the museum as you walk and experience and join and learn about these Americans as they struggled to be free and equal participants in a democracy that continues to challenge that same faith. If we have done our work well, it won't be an easy walk,

---

6   Job 13:15.

it won't be a comfortable walk, but if you look hard enough, it will be a walk that will convince you of the resilience, the hope, the tenacity, and the faith of a people worthy of knowing in the intimate and, yes, triumphant ways we have tried to present them.

If you were at the museum, I would say enjoy, but if that's all you do, we have failed. I'll just say welcome home, because in this place, if you look hard enough, you will find yourself as well. The faith of the museum's ancestors is the faith that believes "there is a fountain filled with blood, / drawn from Immanuel's veins; / and sinners, plunged beneath that flood, / lost all their guilty stains."[7] That is the faith of which I speak.

PRAYER FOR CHARLESTON, SOUTH CAROLINA

REV. KEVIN L. STRICKLAND
EVANGELICAL LUTHERAN CHURCH OF AMERICA

Lord in your mercy, hear our prayer.

O God, you made us in your own image and redeemed us through Jesus your Son. Look with compassion on the whole human family; take away the arrogance and hatred that infect our hearts; break down the walls that separate us; unite us in bonds of love; and through our struggle and confusion, work to accomplish your purposes on earth so that, in your good time, every people and nation may serve you in harmony around your heavenly throne.

Holy One, you do not distance yourself from the pain of your people, but in Jesus, you bear that pain with all who suffer at others' hands. With your cleansing love, bring healing and strength to the people of Mother Emanuel African Methodist Episcopal Church of Charleston, South Carolina, and by your justice, lift them up so that, in body, mind, and spirit, they may again rejoice.

---

7   William Cowper (1731–1800), "There Is a Fountain Filled with Blood."

Out of the darkness, we cry to you, O God. Enable us to find in Christ the faith to trust your care even in the midst of pain. Assure us that we do not walk alone through the valley of the shadow but that your light is leading us into life.

Gracious God, your Son called on you to forgive his enemies while he was suffering shame and death. In these difficult times, lead our enemies and us from prejudice to truth; deliver them and us from hatred, cruelty, and revenge; and in your good time, enable us all to stand reconciled before you. We pray for Dylann Roof, that he may know of your love and find forgiveness in you.

We pray for the Roof family and St. Paul Lutheran Church of Columbia, South Carolina, in their grief.

For the families who grieve for loved ones who were murdered in this senseless tragedy in Charleston, South Carolina, we pray; grant these saints rest eternal, O God, as they now rest in you. We await the day when this world will know of your great shalom and all your saints will be gathered with you.

Into your hands, O God, we commend all for whom we pray, trusting in your mercy, through your Son, Jesus Christ, our Lord.

Amen.

Think about It. Talk about It.

The Knights Party posted the following on their website: "Non-whites who reside in America should be expected to conduct themselves according to Christian principles and must recognize that race mixing is definitely wrong and out of the question. It will be a privilege to live under the authority of a compassionate White Christian government."[8]

How do you feel about this statement?

Where do you see past racial attitudes actively working in today's society?

How does your view of God and faith in Jesus lead you to respond?

---

8   Southern Poverty Law Center, "Knights of the Ku Klux Klan," January 24, 2018, http://www.splcenter.org.

Engage

Henri J. M. Nouwen wrote, "To forget our sins may be an even greater sin than to commit them. Why? Because what is forgotten cannot be healed and that which cannot be healed easily becomes the cause of greater evil."[9]

1. Plan a visit to the National Museum of African American History and Culture.

2. Invite youth and young adults from an ethnically diverse cross-section of churches to work with their shared resources to develop a community mural that depicts their view(s) of the history of race relations in America and Jesus's hope for an authentic Christianity that points to an inclusive, beloved community.

3. Arrange a time and setting to interview and listen to the elders of a black American community. Enrich their talks by building a historical timeline of their families' histories and use online technologies to further document their experiences. If interest and time permit, enlarge the discovery by building a geographical map to explore their families' movements and migration.

   - Discuss what was happening locally, regionally, and nationally across the landscape of their lives.

   - Talk about the ways members of your congregation worked in solidarity with black Americans in their struggles for equality.

   - List the views, beliefs, customs, norms, and laws that were used to either support or challenge the inequalities of their times.

   - Ask the elders to talk about the faith that helped them through the racism they faced.

   - Ask the elders how their memories help shape their outlook on life.

   - Pray about the wounds that require acknowledgement and healing.

---

9   Henri J. M. Nouwen, *The Living Reminder: Service and Prayer in Memory of Jesus Christ* (New York: HarperCollins, 1977), 17.

Go Deeper. Read More.

Milton, A. L. "'Be Reconciled to God!' (2 Cor. 5–20): Biblical Theology and Social Praxis." In *An African Challenge to the Church in the Twenty-First Century.* South Africa: Conference Publication, 1997.

Richards, D. A. J. *Why Love Leads to Justice: Love across the Boundaries.* New York: Cambridge University Press, 2016.

THE BIBLE

But the aim of such instruction is love that comes from a pure heart, a good conscience, and sincere faith. Some people have deviated from these and turned to meaningless talk, desiring to be teachers of the law, without understanding either what they are saying or the things about which they make assertions.

—1 Timothy 1:5–7

Key Term

REVELATION refers to the task of making known what is hidden, of disclosing what is unknown and obscure. The Bible is a source of revealing God's past and continuous acts in the world. Through words, signs, and symbols of the scriptures, people perceive God's desires for all creation.

A Source of Inspiration and Irritation[1]

The Bible sometimes is referred to as the "Book of the Church." It is a source of hope for people whose hope is waning. It provides comfort for those who are desolate. It offers counsel for the confused and guidance for people in need of direction. The promises it presents can encourage people who are despondent. For the Church, the Bible is a timeless treasure.

Yet the Bible, as with many enduring texts, is read, understood, and used in ways that both hurt and heal. The Bible can be a source of irritation as well as a wellspring of inspiration. The Bible becomes a source of irritation when, intentionally and unintentionally, it is dismissive of individual

---

1   This section is based on Joseph V. Crockett, "Engaging Scripture in Everyday Situations," *Black Theology: An International Journal* 3, no. 1 (2004): 97–117.

human worth, denies the equality of all persons, is indifferent to the brokenness of community, or is used to contradict authentic Christianity. The Bible used in acts that lead to such ends becomes complicit in subverting the mission of Jesus of Nazareth, who lived to demonstrate God's unconditional love for the world. The Bible is a source of inspiration when the use of scripture heals rather than harms, builds up rather than destroys, affirms the value and dignity of each person, and is a creative force for human reconciliation and the repair of creation.

> *Scripture affirms our oneness. The distinctions and similarities of theological interpretation within the family of God must be appreciated. . . . No longer can we accept only one dominant theology, which fails to recognize the value of the theologies of others. We worship one and the same God in an enriching variety of ways.*
> —National Council of Churches of Christ in the USA

The Bible in American Life presents a current view of the use of the Bible in the US.[2] It is based on two national surveys. While the Bible is said to be the Book of the Church, slightly more than half of Americans (50.2 percent) read any sacred text outside of worship in the last year.[3] Of the half of the nation that read scripture outside of worship in the last year, "95% named the Bible as the scripture they read."[4]

However the Bible or other sacred texts are used, there is little doubt that there is no contentment when they bring people into contention. The kinds of experiences and levels of knowledge and skill people have influence their capacity for interpreting and understanding the scriptures' meanings in historical and contemporary situations. Awareness of the historical, cultural, geographic, and linguistic subtleties of the words, signs, and symbols of the Bible informs, in obvious and obscure ways, the meanings made by readers, hearers, interpreters, and bystanders.

---

2   Philip Goff, Arthur E. Farnsley II, and Peter J. Thuesen, eds., *The Bible in American Life* (Indianapolis: Indiana University Press, 2014).

3   Goff, Farnsley, and Thuesen, *The Bible in American Life*, 8.

4   Goff, Farnsley, and Thuesen, 7.

*Historically some churches have misused the Great Commission
to "Go into all the world . . ." (Matthew 28: 19) by ignoring
racial ethnic differences.*
—National Council of Churches statement

In addition to knowledge and skills, for the Church, use of the Bible
also requires *faith*, which is understood as convictional knowing, "the
assurance of things hoped for, the conviction of things not seen."[5] Faith
is what is meant when the words of the Bible are held as the "Word of
God." While faith is not to be understood as a substitute for reasoning,
logic, or rational certainty, faith attends to the nonlinguistic dimensions
of human existence. Faith "has a word" that stands in the presence of
human suffering and tragic events and against the tides of meaningless-
ness and hopelessness. Sometimes the word of faith is "Be still and know
that I *am* God."[6] At other times, the word of faith pushes the marginalized to remind the powerful that "even the dogs under the table" have
crumbs to eat.[7]

Faith also is actively involved in the embrace and embodiment of
authentic Christianity. Wayne E. Oates suggests that "the life of faith
is a process whereby integrity of being, simplicity of character, and
wholeness of the expression of life is developed."[8] Allegiance to interpretations and understandings derived from the Bible should involve
deliberative thought in communities where continuous discernment of
potential results of scriptures used to irritate or inspire, to harm or to
heal God's creation is considered. Because racism violates God's intentions of human equality and the wholeness of community, it is a wrong
against God. The Gospel mandate opposes any act, attitude, practice,
process, policy, or system that threatens the wholeness of a person or

---

5   Heb. 11:1.
6   Ps. 46:10.
7   Mark 7:28.
8   Wayne E. Oates, *The Religious Care of the Psychiatric Patient* (Louisville, KY: Westmin-
     ster John Knox, 1990).

community. The privileging of one person, community, or race over another fractures humanity's wholeness.

> *Because racism is a sin against God, we affirm our Gospel mandate to oppose any racist system.*
> —National Council of Churches statement

The Bible on Brokenness among the Races

The Bible is unflinchingly honest in its depiction of human brutality to one another and the brokenness of human society. The enslavement of the Israelites in Egypt, King Herod's slaughter of the children of Bethlehem, an innocent man tortured and executed by crucifixion—the Bible is full of human suffering, pain, and grief. Yet it is also filled with hope for a new day and the faith that God's way is one of transformation and triumph:

Through him [Jesus], God was pleased to reconcile to himself all things, whether on earth or in heaven, by making peace through the blood of his cross. And you who were once estranged and hostile in mind, doing evil deeds, he has now reconciled in his fleshly body through death, so as to present you holy and blameless and irreproachable before him.[9]

Here Paul defines God's call to us to live lives transformed by Christ's redeeming and reconciling transformation of the universe—systemic reconciliation. Reconciliation is first God's action, God's initiative. When humanity was hostile to one another and to God, God reached out decisively in Christ to reconcile us to the Creator and to call us to a new relationship with one another.

Human life has often been torn by strife and filled with hurt and misunderstanding. Christ's life shows us what life is intended to be: oneness with each other, with the universe, and with God. Christ's reconciling

9   Col. 1:20–22.

work has opened the door to the vocation of a holy life. We believe that Christ's life, death, and resurrection offer the fullest expression of the authentic life that His followers—Christians—are to embody. We are called to live in peace with one another, treating one another as sisters and brothers in the body of Christ that is the Church. A message and ministry of reconciliation is entrusted to us. As Christians, this is our call, our vocation, and our purpose for living. "Be reconciled to God"[10] is a plea, an invitation, and a call to action. To acknowledge Christ's reconciling work is to speak words of reconciliation to one another and to build bridges of reconciliation, to love, to provide safety and protection for the vulnerable and oppressed, and to live freely in the hope Christ offers.

This is not an abstract call to Christians. Paul through the letter to the Colossians directly addresses each of *us* ("*you* who were once estranged and hostile in mind"). The call to claim the reconciliation Christ offers and gives comes to us individually—and together as the Church. He calls us to conversion of our minds, hearts, and actions. If we accept that call, it allows Christ's transformative power to expose and convert the evil in each of us and within our community. Through the Spirit, we become part of Christ's cosmic work of redemption!

So we live in between the already and the not yet. Called by Christ to be a holy and blameless people, how do we show that we are already a reconciled community in Christ? How do we break the injustices and prejudices pervading our minds, thoughts, and actions both as individuals and as communities? How do we live before Christ, "in his presence, in his service, [and] under his care,"[11] to allow Christ to do His reconciling work in us and through us, reaching out in love and service to others, particularly those who do not look like us?

---

10   2 Cor. 5:20.
11   Markus Barth, Helmut Blanke, and Astrid B. Beck, *Colossians: A New Translation with Introduction and Commentary* (New York: Doubleday, 1994), 223.

Think about It. Talk about It.
How do you understand the messages of the scriptures?
What guidelines does your community use to interpret the meanings
of passages that appear to be in conflict with other scriptures or
your view of God?
How is God working in your own heart around issues of race?
What has been your experience(s) of race that challenges the Church's
witness as an inclusive, beloved community?

Engage
Read Philemon. Discuss the letter from the perspective of the major
characters and the Christians in Philemon's house.

1. What are the aims and hopes of Paul, the writer of the letter?
2. What challenges does Paul's letter present Philemon?
3. What threats, opportunities, and feelings might Onesimus experience?
4. Paul also writes to the church in Philemon's house; what are its
   opportunities and obligations?
5. What, if any, similarities and responsibilities might your church
   face today? How can you respond?

Go Deeper. Read More.
Blount, Brian K., and Cain Hope Felder, eds. *True to Our Native Land:
An African American New Testament Commentary.* Minneapolis, MN:
Fortress, 2007.
Bovati, Pietro, and Fr. Michael J. Smith. *Re-establishing Justice: Legal
Terms, Concepts, and Procedures in the Hebrew Bible.* London: T&T
Clark, 2017.
Felder, Cain Hope, ed. *Stony the Road We Trod: African American Bibli-
cal Interpretation.* Minneapolis, MN: Fortress, 1991.
Page, Huge R., Jr. *The Africana Bible: Reading Israel's Scriptures from
Africa and the African Diaspora.* Minneapolis, MN: Fortress, 2010.

THE SEARCH
FOR JUSTICE

O Lord, how long shall the wicked,
how long shall the wicked exult?

They pour out their arrogant words;
all the evildoers boast.

They crush your people, O Lord,
and afflict your heritage.

They kill the widow and the stranger,
they murder the orphan,

and they say, "The Lord does not see;
the God of Jacob does not perceive."

—Psalm 94:3–7

Key Terms

EXCOMMUNICATION describes the formal act of suspending, expelling, or restricting the rights of a member from affiliation with an organization.

REPARATION refers to the making of amends for a wrong by the person or group who has committed the injurious act.

SOLIDARITY refers to unity that produces or is based on common interests, standards, sympathies, objectives, or vision. A Christian view of solidarity is not homogeneity, unity based on sameness or uniformity. Rather, a Christian understanding of solidarity is related to the transformative and transforming agency of Jesus Christ.

Systemic refers to that which relates, pertains to, or affects the whole. Racism not only pertains to individual biases, prejudices, and hate; it also pertains to the organizational processes that maintain the enterprise.

> *To correct the system of unequal justice, we must challenge every decision-maker to be responsible for fairness and dignity towards others with measurable actions. In turn, we must use our collective voices to give voice to the voiceless.*
> —James Bell, *The Covenant with Black America*

Racism, as an appropriation of prejudice with power, exists in opposition to an inclusive, beloved community. The integrity of authentic Christianity is revealed as an inclusive, beloved community. The values of both an authentic Christianity and an inclusive, beloved community include love, justice, freedom, security, and peace. These values are consistent with the life of Jesus. An inclusive, beloved community supports people's opportunities to thrive. Racism threatens community. It fractures neighborhoods and divides the nation.

The deeply entrenched structures of systemic racism and white privilege defy easy fixes. Remedies need to provide redress for the past and implement a more just future. Let's look at five options and consider what they might accomplish.

> *The Church also exists to teach the law of God, announcing that the God who justifies expects all people to do justice.*
> —Evangelical Lutheran Church in America statement

Apologies

Apologies are complicated. In litigious American society, to apologize is to make oneself vulnerable to legal action, to being sued for damages. Even when wrongdoing is known, Americans are often afraid of the consequences of admitting it. Yet as conflict expert Donna Hicks points out, "When we have been harmed, especially under circumstances that feel unjust, we have a need for public acknowledgement of the pain and suffering that was caused."[1] Formal public statements of apology can sometimes offer the acknowledgement and affirmation that people need to move forward—whether or not the apology is accepted. For example, the United Church of Canada offered a formal apology to Canadian Indigenous peoples in 1986. The National Native Council of the United Church officially received the apology without accepting it. This was a mutual recognition of the deep harm that had been done. That recognition began a long process toward healing.[2]

Those harmed by systemic oppression may legitimately feel that an apology is merely cheap talk. In response to a white theology professor's apology for his participation in the system of apartheid in a gathering of church leaders in 1991 in South Africa, a black participant responded, "I don't want nice apologies so white people can feel good. What I want is for whites to join us in the struggle to dismantle apartheid and create justice."[3] The apology as given was rejected, though the rejection came with a challenge to transform it from meaningless words into meaningful action.

Apologies can be a step in acknowledging that deep and lasting harm has been inflicted upon an individual or a people. When white Americans can really hear the pain and lament of people of color, both from historical experiences and ongoing realities of oppression, an apology can be a starting point for deeper understanding and honest conversation. An apology must be contextually specific and reflect authentic regret. It must be based on an established relationship so that the people apologizing have credibility for making the apology. And it must offer a commitment to a changed heart and action. When these conditions are present, an apology may have significant meaning for all involved. The work cannot end there, however. The next step must be for those who have apologized to join the struggle to create justice.

1   Donna Hicks, *Dignity: Its Essential Role in Resolving Conflicts* (New Haven, CT: Yale University Press, 2011), 187.
2   Walter Wink, *When the Powers Fall: Reconciliation in the Healing of Nations* (Minneapolis, MN: Fortress, 1998), 55.
3   Wink, 28.

Resolutions of Solidarity

The test of every institution or policy is whether it enhances or threatens human life and dignity.
    —Archbishop John Roach, *Songs of Joy* by Joan Chittister

Formal statements of solidarity go beyond apology. Where apologies focus on the hurts of the past, a resolution of solidarity offers constructive steps to change a system of injustice. The Governing Board of the National Council of Churches adopted a statement on Kanaka Maoli sovereignty in Hawaii in 1993. That statement, "A Stolen Nation," identified the cause of the plight of the Maolis as the "sin of racism" and the "genocide of the Indigenous people of Hawai'i." The resolution called for a "process of seeking justice for the Kanaka Maoli and reconciliation between the Kanaka Maoli and the international Christian community." It further called on "member communions to bear witness and seek forgiveness" and listed five specific ways to "support the Kanaka Maoli and their right to regain their sovereignty."[4] Standing in solidarity requires more than resolutions; it requires a willingness to take action for justice.

Racial justice is recognizing our oneness in Christ, confessing that we have not become what God wants us to be, and committing ourselves to pressing on to that mark of high calling by which we can become a liberating symbol to our nation and world of what it means to be the people of God. In so doing, we can challenge our nation to live up to its high purposes. We can challenge all the nations to take seriously the struggle for the freedom and peace of all humankind.
    —American Baptist Churches in the USA statement

---

4   National Council of Churches of Christ in the USA, "A Stolen Nation—Kanaka Maoli Sovereignty," November 11, 1993, http://pjrcpeace.org/19._STOLEN_NATION_NCCCUSA.html.

Reparations or Restitution

Deeply wounded individuals and groups cannot move toward a transformed future without redress of injuries. The question of restitution asks what needs to be paid back or restored to those who have been wronged and establishes what compensation they deserve.[5] It is not possible through monetary payment to compensate adequately for the physical, emotional, familial, and societal suffering that black Americans have endured through United States history. Still, reparations are an acknowledgement of past damage and deprivation.[6] They are a form of tangible repentance for sins of the past, and they offer reparatory justice. In the United States, the Civil Liberties Act of 1988 officially apologized to Japanese Americans for internment during World War II. It also authorized the payment of reparations to those individuals still living who had been interned. No form of reparation for slavery and discrimination has been provided to black Americans. The National African American Reparations Commission (NAARC) has proposed a ten-point reparation plan to redress the evils of the African Holocaust—the Trans-Atlantic Slave Trade/Middle Passage—and the five hundred years of imperialism and colonialism people of African heritage have collectively suffered:

1. A formal apology and the establishment of a Maafa/African Holocaust institute[7]
2. The right of reparation and creation of an African knowledge program.
3. The right to land for social and economic development
4. Funds for cooperative enterprises and socially responsible entrepreneurial development

---

5   Jill Stauffer, *Ethical Loneliness: The Injustice of Not Being Heard* (New York: Columbia University Press, 2015), 144.

6   See Edward E. Baptist, *The Half Has Never Been Told: Slavery and the Making of American Capitalism* (New York: Basic Books, 2014); Jennifer Harvey, *Dear White Christians: For Those Still Longing for Racial Reconciliation* (Grand Rapids, MI: Eerdmans, 2014).

7   *Maafa*, also known as the African Holocaust, is a Kiswahili term for disaster, calamity, or terrible occurrence. This term has been used to describe the Trans-Atlantic Slave Trade/Middle Passage.

5. Resources for the health, wellness, and healing of black families and communities
6. Education for community development and empowerment
7. Affordable housing for healthy black communities and wealth generation
8. Strengthening black America's information and communications infrastructure
9. Preserving black sacred sites and monuments
10. Repairing the damages of the "Criminal Injustice System"[8]

A Truth and Reconciliation Commission

Some communities and nations have set up truth and reconciliation commissions based on the model created by Archbishop Desmond Tutu in South Africa to address wounds of the apartheid era. In a *Washington Post* opinion piece published soon after the 2017 Charlottesville, Virginia, white supremacy rally, former congressman Tom Perriello called for a truth and reconciliation commission on race in Virginia to find a common historical narrative, address how that history is memorialized, and seek "policy reforms that address the painful legacies of our past." Perriello argued that such a commission would serve to "work across deep fault lines of conflicting narratives to establish common ground and common facts."[9]

Such commissions are a form of transitional justice. Philosopher Jill Stauffer explains that they function "in a present moment, to revise memory or experience of a past, with the hope of opening up a future not fully determined by past harms."[10] The Truth and Reconciliation Commission of Canada might serve as a model for a prospective truth and

---

8   The Institute of the Black World 21st Century, "NAARC Rolls Out Preliminary 10-Point Reparations Plan at Congressional Black Caucus Conference, 2015," April 16, 2015, https://ibw21.org/initiative-posts/naarc-posts/naarc-rolls-out-preliminary-10-point-reparations-plan/.
9   Tom Perriello, "Virginia Needs a Truth and Reconciliation Commission on Race," *Washington Post*, September 6, 2017, https://www.washingtonpost.com/opinions/virginia-needs-a-truth-and-reconciliation-commission-on-race/2017/09/06/8f1a5bde-8e6d-11e7-8df5-c2e5cf46c1e2_story.html?utm_term=.229fee316926.
10   Stauffer, *Ethical Loneliness*, 113.

reconciliation process on racial issues in the United States. The Canadian commission worked from 2008 to 2015 to document abuses in Indian residential schools and to try to establish relationships of mutual understanding and respect between Aboriginal peoples and other Canadians. The Indian Residential Schools Survivors Committee served as the advisory body. In contrast with Archbishop Desmond Tutu's Truth and Reconciliation Commission in South Africa, the Canadian commission was not a criminal tribunal to convene hearings. Rather, it focused on truth-telling, particularly on hearing the victims' stories. Some observers wrote afterward that truth and reconciliation is not about "forgive and forget"; rather, it is about "remember and change."[11]

These commissions work at achieving reconciliation for collective guilt; their effectiveness at healing the individual wounds of past injury is questionable. Studies warn that personal testimony may reawaken trauma in the victims rather than facilitate healing.[12] For constitutional reasons, it would be difficult in the United States for churches to be involved in a government-sponsored national or state truth and reconciliation process. But the churches could take leadership in designing and offering safe truth-telling spaces and a process that could lead to a clearer acknowledgement of past abuses and serve as a catalyst for positive change.

Excommunication
Episcopal priest Jabriel Ballentine argues that a clergyperson has a moral obligation to confront a known white supremacist member of the congregation and call that person to repentance. If the parishioner refuses to change, then, Ballentine says, the minister must excommunicate that person in order to excise the "cancer" of racism from the parish. The church "cannot be complicit in racism, bigotry, and hatred,"

11   Quoted in Brian Rice and Anna Snyder, "Reconciliation in the Context of a Settler Society: Healing the Legacy of Colonialism in Canada," in *"Speaking My Truth": Reflections on Reconciliation and Residential School*, ed. Shelagh Rogers, Mike DeGagné, Jonathan Dewar, and Glen Lowry (Aboriginal Healing Foundation, 2012), 47, http://speakingmytruth.ca/downloads/AHFvol1/04_Rice_Snyder.pdf.
12   Stauffer, *Ethical Loneliness*, 54.

Fr. Ballentine insists, "and if the church will not stand up against these now, it should close down."[13] Fr. Ballentine's argument that known racists should be barred from receiving the Eucharist is controversial. Yet his call to Christians to speak and act against the sin of racial bigotry is compelling, particularly in light of the church's complicity in segregation and continuing racial injustice.

The prophet Amos declares that worship, sacrifice, and pilgrimage festivals mean nothing if our lives do not express God's justice: "Let justice roll down like waters, and righteousness like an ever-flowing stream."[14] Fr. Ballentine's call is made in this prophetic spirit.

PRAYER FOR HOPE AND COMFORT FOR THE MARGINALIZED AND OPPRESSED

EBONY J. GRISOM
AMERICAN BAPTIST CHURCHES

God of justice, this world is rife with injustice. We live in the manifestations of fallen humanity daily. Longing for Eden's perfection, we torture ourselves and one another with ever-present sin. Systemic racism runs rampant everywhere, including in the church. We have been mistaken for the serpent. We are not the enemy: we are brothers and sisters. We are made in your image. We are included in the sheep of your pasture, yet others seek to scatter and destroy us. We pray that You would be the shepherd that You have promised in Your Word as spoken through the prophet Jeremiah: "Then I myself will gather the remnant of my flock out of the lands where I have driven them, and I will bring them back to their fold, and they shall be fruitful and multiply. I will raise up shepherds over them who will shepherd them, and

---

13   Fr. Jabriel Ballentine and Fr. Cayce Ramey, "Excommunicating White Supremacy—Redeeming the Church," *Racial Heresy* podcast, August 23, 2017, https://www.blubrry.com/racial_heresy/.

14   Amos 5:24.

they shall not fear any longer, or be dismayed, nor shall any be missing, says the Lord."[15] Therein lies our hope. Hallelujah! Finally, we will be emancipated from the marginalized earthly existence and called to live into the exceedingly abundant bounty that You intended in the beginning. As you hasten Your coming, quicken us to create a world where this just reality reigns on earth. "Thy kingdom come, Thy will be done, on earth as it is in heaven . . ." Make us one in the Spirit. We pray in the name of the Father, Son, and Holy Spirit. Amen.

A LITANY FOR THE REPAIR OF THE WORLD

REV. DR. TAMMY WIENS
ASSOCIATE FOR CHRISTIAN FORMATION
NATIONAL OFFICE OF THE PRESBYTERIAN CHURCH (USA)

Tikkun olam (תיקון עולם)

In Jewish tradition, *tikkun olam* ("repair of the world") is a conviction that our obedience to God's commandments will advance God's own action in perfecting all of creation. The concept of *tikkun olam* aligns with Jesus's teaching on the Great Commandment in the Gospels. As Christians live out their obedience to "love the Lord God with all our heart, soul, mind, and strength" and to "love the neighbor as self," we too usher in the reign of God and help repair the world.

ONE: Healing God, prompt our eagerness to do good in the world.
MANY: May God's peace and justice flow through me.

ONE: Hear our hopes for a world in which people of every color embrace one another as brothers and sisters.
MANY: May God's peace and justice flow through me.

---

15   Jer. 23:3–4.

ONE: Make our hearts tender to the "other," so that we see every stranger as a potential friend.
MANY: May God's peace and justice flow through me.

ONE: Relieve our fears of war and terrorism and stir in us a prayer for our "enemies."
MANY: May God's peace and justice flow through me.

ONE: Expose the lies that pit neighbor against neighbor, Republican against Democrat, Christian against Muslim or Jew, us against them. Bring Your truth to light so that we might live peaceably with one another.
MANY: May God's peace and justice flow through me.

ONE: Renew our sense of Sabbath, where one day of honoring You brings all other days of the week into alignment with Your sacred purpose for all of life.
MANY: May God's peace and justice flow through me.

ALL: Lord God, hear our prayer for the repair of the world. Bring healing to all people of every tribe and nation so that we might live in peace and unity under Your good and perfect reign.

PRAYER OF HOPE

KATHRYN MARY LOHRE
EVANGELICAL LUTHERAN CHURCH IN AMERICA

Good and gracious God,
You have set us free from the slavery of our sin, including the sin of racism.
You have gathered your church together, united and freed in Christ.
You have bestowed us with treasures of diversity, blessings that too often we bend into burdens.

For we cling to—all of us, whether captivated by or held captive to—the sin of racism. This deadly "mix of power, privilege, and prejudice" keeps us divided from each other and from you.[16]

O God, our God, we cry out to you that black lives matter.

We come before you, as the prophet Amos did in his time, calling out for your justice to roll down like waters. We cry out for the black lives that are degraded, diminished, demonized, divided, and destroyed, for as long as one cannot breathe, none of us can. The body of Christ is suffocating, and the church is complicit. Breathe your breath of life into us afresh.

Give us your wisdom to help us understand the complexity of racism and the compounding nature of oppressions. Give us your courage in our homes, schools, and communities as we teach our children to honor each person as made in your image. Give us your Pentecost vision of God's people once scattered now gathered together as we seek to change and build more equitable systems and structures for all.[17]

We are your people of hope—incarnate, *in the flesh*—that God is with us, *Emmanuel. This* is the "hope that does not disappoint us."[18] This is the hope we long to embody to your world. In Jesus's name, Amen.

A PRAYER FOR STRENGTH

REV. KAREN GEORGIA A. THOMPSON
UNITED CHURCH OF CHRIST

O Lord, how long shall I cry for help, and you will not listen? Or cry to you "Violence!" and you will not save?[19]

---

16   Evangelical Lutheran Church in America, *"Freed in Christ, Race, Ethnicity, and Culture"* (ELCA Social Statement, 1993).
17   John 11:52.
18   Rom. 5:5.
19   Hab. 1:2.

God of presence and hope, hear our cries and our longing for hope and peace in a world where injustice is rampant. You made all people in your image, an array of diverse beauty, a reflection of your love for us, the manifestation of your presence. You formed us to live life abundantly and to share freely the resources you gave to us.

Our cries are loud and our tears flow deeply as we weep amid the pain of generational racial injustices and the degradation of the human spirit and for the lives broken and cast down because of racism. We cry amid the suffering and despair; we cry because the fear that lives among us creeps across the land destroying lives.

God, we have failed to show love to our neighbor. We have withheld compassion and care in times of need. We have neglected to see you in the face and spirits of those with whom we live. We have created divisions and stratifications that justify the dehumanization of some while falsely elevating the lives and worth of others. Forgive us, Holy One.

The sin of racism lives among us and continues to be a source of deep wounding and division. We cry out to you with the memories of those who have gone before us. Our tears for their pain are still wet on our faces as we cry out anew in these days, as we experience pain and suffering because of the color of our skin. We know that we too are the image of you. Let justice roll down among us in this land.

Restore our souls, Creator God. Help us create new ways of bringing justice, peace, and unity among us.

Renew our spirits, Breath of Life. Help us remain unfailing in our quest to see all people living in freedom, safety, and humane conditions with dignity and possibility.

Revive our strength, Living Water. Help us walk with boldness and courage in these days as we move toward a vision that is daunting yet attainable. We will not rest, O God, until all are fully free.

Hear us now, we pray. Grant us your peace, your hope, your love. Amen.

PRAYER INSPIRED BY THE BOOK OF HABAKKUK

REV. KATHRYN BROWN
AFRICAN METHODIST EPISCOPAL ZION CHURCH

How long, O Lord, must my people endure racial oppression and injustice? How long must we try to make sense of senseless actions by those who are supposed to protect us? How many times can we be disappointed over unjust decisions by a justice system that continues to fail us?

I cry out to You in distress over the injustices that continue to plague my people. Why, O God, is there no justice? Why do You allow wrongdoing to continue and allow those who do wrong to go free? My sons are shot like hogs in the street, and there is no justice. Innocent children witness their fathers killed by those who are called to protect them, and there is no justice. I cry out to You, Lord God, because it seems that the law is paralyzed. Destruction and violence are before us. Strife and conflict abound. It seems that we are going backward instead of moving forward. The wicked go free while the innocent are made into villains. Mothers bury their sons hoping that there will be justice. Fathers are in anguish because they cannot find justice for their sons and daughters, whose lives just do not seem to matter.

In the midst of my despair, I am reminded that You, my God, are sovereign. You are from everlasting to everlasting. You heard the cry of my ancestors, and You hear my cry. You delivered my forefathers and foremothers, and I trust You to deliver this generation. Although our enemies seem to prevail, grant us courage. Grant us wisdom. Deliver us from the evils of racism. Open the eyes of the blind. Grant us grace to trust You. Change the hearts of the wicked. Let the righteous never lose hope. In Jesus's name, Amen.

EQUITY PRAYER

B. MICHAEL WATSON, BISHOP
THE UNITED METHODIST CHURCH

Gracious and merciful God, whose divine and wondrous love is so freely poured upon us all, help us be united by that graceful love. We pray for peace, justice, and equality among all people. Teach us to be more and more like you and show no distinction among races, nations, and other people groups because you have created each of us in your image and as your beloved family. We are your family. You are Lord of all, and your impartial generosity is mercifully shown to all who will receive it.

Save us by your grace. Draw us together in Christ-like love for all our sisters and brothers of every race and tribe upon this earth you so lovingly created.

Bridge our divisions by cleansing our hearts from sin, hatred, and warring madness so that truly there may be equal justice and mercy for all.

We know that Christ is not to be divided but rather was sent to reconcile all of us to you, O God. In the precious name of Jesus, our Savior, let us praise your holy name by being reconciled to you and to each other and become ambassadors of your love, mercy, and grace.

In Jesus Christ's name we pray. Amen.

Truth-Telling Prayer

Elizabeth Eaton, Bishop
Evangelical Lutheran Church in America

Again I saw all the oppressions that are practiced under the sun. Look—the tears of the oppressed—with no one to comfort them! On the side of their oppressors there was power—with no one to comfort them.[20]

God, our creator, out of love and for love you made us. We are all the work of your hands. We walk the same earth and breathe the same air, and yet . . .

God of righteousness, it is your will that all people live in equity and peace, that all have a share in your abundant life, that there is liberty and justice for all, and yet . . .

God of life, you claimed us in baptism, buried us with Christ in a death like his, and promised to unite us with Christ in a resurrection like his. We have already died the only death that really matters, and yet . . .

We do not recognize the full humanity in others. There is not justice for all. In our fear, we doubt the resurrection.

The hard work of truth-telling—and truth-hearing—is set before us. The painful reality that racial equity does not exist in our nation or our church cannot be ignored. Help us resist any rush to reconciliation before repentance. The oppressed will not be comforted until their voices are heard. The oppressors will find no comfort until they relinquish power.

In your love, compassionate God, keep us in this tension. In your severe mercy, use this pain to bring action and change. We pray this through Christ, our Lord, in whom the dividing wall of hostility has already been broken down. Amen.

---

20   Eccles. 4:1.

PRAYER OF JUSTICE FOR RACIAL EQUITY

MARY ELIZABETH MOORE, PHD
BOSTON UNIVERSITY SCHOOL OF THEOLOGY

Holy, Merciful, and Just God,

We come before You in deep sorrow for the many ways our human family has fallen short of holiness, mercy, and justice; for the many ways our churches have fallen short; for the many ways we *ourselves* have fallen short, dishonoring the blessings of others, otherness, and difference. God, have mercy on us!

Open our visions to the wide horizons of *Your* vision of justice and grant us courage to act for justice in all aspects of our personal, communal, societal, and global lives. God, have mercy on us!

Guide us even as we falter and fail. Fill us with strength for the long, persistent journey toward justice.

O God, who makes all things new, who makes promises again and again!

You told people of old, "I am about to do a new thing; now it springs forth, do You not perceive it? I will make a way in the wilderness and rivers in the desert."[21]

We confess that we have not trusted Your promises. We are locked into patterns of racist thinking and racist structures that we accept, sometimes by intentional or unintentional ignorance, sometimes by a sense of superiority or despair.

We do not trust that You *really are about to do a new thing* and that Your new thing requires us to be open to change. It requires our willingness to confess, repent, and turn around. We come before You with our fears that we are not able to risk change, even change in the persistent patterns that distort our very souls.

---

21   Isa. 43:19.

God, have mercy on us, and open us to the "new thing" that You are doing, making a just way in spite of our unwillingness to trust, awakening us to our racial thinking and action, and offering us promises and strength to travel this long justice journey.

God of the justice journey, who showed the way in Jesus!

Jesus was open to change, even in his encounter with a Syrophoenician woman who challenged his unwillingness to cast a demon from her daughter, simply because she was Syrophoenician. Jesus responded to the challenge with a pause and then a change: "For saying that, you may go—the demon has left your daughter."[22]

We confess that we have not opened ourselves to the radical justice of Jesus, or even the radical justice of many forebears, or even our own potential to do justice, with the help of Your Spirit.

Grant us a vision for racial-ethnic-human shalom/salaam! Grant us courage to face the ugliness of racism in ourselves and our communities! Grant us trust in Your Spirit to create a way toward justice and to travel with us, toward a world where *You* are about to do a very new thing with our very human selves, and by the power of Your justice-bearing grace! Amen!

Think about It. Talk about It.

A statement many black Americans commonly hear from whites is, "If we knew what they wanted, we could help them in their struggles for justice and equality." Review and discuss the ten-point proposal articulated by the National African American Reparations Commission.

What is your reaction to these demands as an act of repentance for "America's original sin"—racism?

Which, if any, concerns are you willing to work toward overcoming together with whites, blacks, and other people of color?

---

22   Mark 7:29. Narrative in Mark 7:24–30; Matt. 15:21–28.

Engage
1. Host a dialogue with religious, political, and business leaders in your community. Engage them in a discussion on reparations—what it would involve, the opportunities and challenges it presents to churches in your area and your community.
2. Arrange for and fund an interracial study group to learn about Georgetown University's program of reparation within its institutional mission and purpose. Conduct an online search, "Georgetown University Working Group on Slavery, Memory, and Reconciliation." Identify and commit to three or four actionable outcomes as a result of the study.

Go Deeper. Read More.
Douglas, Kelly Brown. *Stand Your Ground: Black Bodies and the Justice of God.* Maryknoll, NY: Orbis Books, 2015.
Hayner, Priscilla B. *Unspeakable Truth: Facing the Challenge of Truth Commissions.* London: Routledge, 2002.

THE PRICE OF
JUSTICE AND
ITS COST TO US

He called the crowd with his disciples, and said to them, "If any want to become my followers, let them deny themselves and take up their cross and follow me."
—Mark 8:34

Key Terms

CHANGE refers to the act of making something different from what it is or would be if left unattended.

TRANSFORMATION connotes something more than mere change. It conveys a deep alteration in form and structure—a metamorphism.

VOCATION is a summons to a life with God in relationship with others that involves the use of one's time, talents, and treasures in whatever setting one is in. It assumes that life has purpose and that God is involved in a person's purpose, actively inviting a commitment to a particular path or way of life.

Recessions and recoveries come and go, while whole communities of people are left behind, never enjoying "recovery," in predominantly black and brown neighborhoods across the country. Law enforcement is then expected to control or at least contain the predictable outcomes of poverty's chaos, pain, anger, and hopelessness in those black and brown neighborhoods, while the rest of us evade our responsibility to end that poverty and hopelessness . . .
—Jim Wallis, *America's Original Sin*

Conversations on racial justice and discussions of remedies are painful and difficult. Racial understanding in America is stymied by passionately held perspectives and conflicting convictions. Differing belief systems are reflected in competing movements: Black Lives Matter, Blue Lives Matter, All Lives Matter, and White Lives Matter. Disputes over Confederate monuments are symbols of American history. Like any symbol, they evoke differing interpretations that are informed by the memories of ancestors across the years. One's own experiences in job searches, medical care, and housing shape perceptions of fairness or racial disparities in these important aspects of life.

> *It's past time to act on race. We would not continually have Fergusons and Baltimores if it were not for racism.*
> —African Methodist Episcopal Church statement

The evils of slavery, Reconstruction, generations of segregation, and Jim Crow set in motion long-lasting repercussions of systemic racism and discrimination for black Americans. That perception is not an alternate history; it is a history woven into the fabric of American society. "You can't ask for reconciliation but continue the power structures of white power and the language of white privilege," theologian Loida I. Martell argues. "To talk about reconciliation and sin, you have to sit at the table with those who are being historically victimized. We can't sit at the table unless we sit at the table as equals. What does that take? What do I have to give up in order to sit at the table as your equal? That's where the conversation gets more serious."[1]

> *Christians must acknowledge that, despite their good intentions, religious and societal structures, institutions and systems can and do perpetuate racism. They must confess that by its style of*

---

1   Loida I. Martell, plenary conversation, National Council of Churches Faith and Order Convening Table, May 13, 2017.

organization and management the white institutional church
excludes those who are victims of racism.
—National Council of Churches statement

For black Americans, other people of color, and whites to become an inclusive, beloved community will require change. Change is the price churches and communities striving for an authentic Christianity will have to pay to become an inclusive, beloved community. John P. Kotter identifies eight important steps that are necessary in order to initiate and sustain such an organizational revolution:

1. Establish a sense of urgency.
2. Form a powerful coalition.
3. Create a vision.
4. Communicate the vision.
5. Empower others to act on the vision.
6. Plan and create short-term wins.
7. Consolidate improvements and continue more change.
8. Institutionalize new approaches.[2]

While the details of Kotter's insights are worth fuller explanation, taking common sense steps on the list he offers can help churches unite against racism. Kotter's recommendations can equip good-willed individuals to work collectively to dismantle the structural building blocks of racism and to move closer to achieving the kind and quality of community God envisions for the world.

> *We have confused justice and charity. Charity was always con-*
> *sidered the highest virtue. . . . The spiritual trap was that we*
> *always remained in charge; we decided who was worthy and*

---

2   John P. Kotter, "Leading Change: The Eight Steps to Transformation," in *The Leader's Change Handbook: An Essential Guide to Setting Direction and Taking Action*, ed. Jay A. Conger, Gretchen M. Spreitzer, and Edward E. Lawler III (San Francisco: Jossey-Bass, 1999), 87–99.

unworthy of our love, and we garnered significant self-esteem as
a byproduct. The question then becomes: Is it any type of surren-
der or just another type of control? Are we instruments of God's
love flowing into this world, or are we perhaps inhibiting that
flow by our lack of true solidarity?

—Richard Rohr, *Grace in Action*

While it is necessary to know what transformative change requires,
it is also helpful to understand the forces and barriers that keep change
from taking place. Michael Beer provides an initial list of barriers to
consider:

- Unclear strategy and conflicting priorities
- Ineffective leadership
- Top-down, hierarchical, or laissez-faire approaches
- Poor coordination and teamwork across distinct units of the group
- Poor communication between leaders and members
- Lack of preparedness in terms of knowledge, skills, and abilities to
  enact the change sought[3]

Whites, blacks, and all people of color must sit at the table together
in candid conversations, acknowledging America's history and our current plight to take up collective action in order to forge a new trajectory
away from racial hostility, discrimination, and division. This requires
white Americans to give up an uncritical and often glorified story of the
United States as a place that embraces and fully integrates minorities.[4]
In order to engage in conversations about race with people of color,

---

3   Michael Beer, "Leading Learning and Learning to Lead: An Action Learning
     Approach to Developing Organizational Fitness," in *The Leader's Change Handbook:*
     An Essential Guide to Setting Direction and Taking Action, ed. Jay A. Conger, Gretchen
     M. Spreitzer, and Edward E. Lawler III (San Francisco: Jossey-Bass, 1999), 144.
4   See Douglas A. Foster, "The White Church and White Supremacy: How White
     Christians Created and Perpetuate the Ideology of White Supremacy," in *Thinking*
     Theologically about Mass Incarceration, ed. Antonios Kireopoulos, Mitzi J. Budde, and
     Matthew D. Lundberg (Mahwah, NJ: Paulist Press, 2017), 43–80.

white people must bring awareness to the table in addition to good will. Whites need to be open to hearing new perspectives and to learning about black experiences, histories, and cultures, particularly, in the words of African American studies professor Dr. Joseph Thompson, "the depths of the injustices experienced by people of color and the heights of the resistance, resilience, and ingenuity shown by people of color under unjust conditions."[5] A genuine conversation can commence when whites begin a process of inner transformation in how they view and relate to persons of color.

Racial justice can only be achieved by an honest reappraisal of the past and a willingness to embrace the other in order to bring about a just and lasting place for black Americans and other minorities in American society. To sit at the table as equals, to give up the certainty of being right, and to pursue together the work for racial healing requires courage, humility, and integrity as well as faith, hope, and love. These are signs of authentic Christianity.

PRAYER OF REPENTANCE

LAUREN R. HOLDER
ST. LUKE'S EPISCOPAL CHURCH

God of justice, send your Holy Spirit to assist us in the difficult and sacred work of repentance. Shine your light and your love on the darkest corners of our hearts, that we may rid ourselves of the sin of racism. Restore us to our whole selves that we may be able to serve Christ in all persons. And rescue us from complacency that we may be compelled to action, until all are truly free. Amen.

---

5   Joseph Downing Thompson, director of Multicultural Ministries and visiting professor of African American Studies, Virginia Theological Seminary, private email correspondence, November 22, 2017.

A Commissioning of Community

Triune God, you are perfect community. Heal the fractures in and among ourselves that together we may go out into the world proclaiming a love that hides from nothing. Bless these persons with the courage and endurance needed to proclaim the Gospel of peace. Give them joy in their work, patience with themselves and each other, and boldness in their daily walk with You. In the name of the Father, and of the Son, and of the Holy Spirit. Amen.

THAT WE MAY BE ONE . . . (FOR REAL)

REV. DENISE JANSSEN, PhD
SAMUEL DEWITT SCHOOL OF THEOLOGY
VIRGINIA UNION UNIVERSITY

A key part of Jesus's fervent prayer for his disciples in the Gospel of John chapter 17 is that they would be one. In verses 20–23, as part of his chapters-long prayer in the last half of John's gospel, Jesus says,

I ask not only on behalf of these, but also on behalf of those who will believe in me through their word, that they may all be one. As you, Father, are in me and I am in you, may they also be in us, so that the world may believe that you have sent me. The glory that you have given me I have given them, so that they may be one, as we are one, I in them and you in me, that they may become completely one, so that the world may know that you have sent me and have loved them even as you have loved me.[6]

People of faith understand reconciliation is a key part of our discipleship. That reconciliation is not superficial, not cheap. It comes at a

---

6   John 17:20–23.

great cost, and the reconciliation for which we strive must be genuine.
And so today we pray:

Holy One, hear the prayers of your children
who seek to be one
in truth and in love.
We do not know exactly what we are asking,
what it will cost, but
we know this unity was so important to Jesus
that he prayed fervently
in his last days
that we might experience it.
Sculpt us.
Carve us.
Whittle us.
Fashion us, your people,
removing in one area and building up in another,
that we might be one.
Give us courage to see that which *must go* in order for unity to come:
privilege, greed, hatred, jealousy,
the long-held scars that must be softened.
Give us passion for the journey of reconciliation,
which necessarily leads through shadowy places in us.
And mark us first
and always
with your love,
that we may be yours,
and through unity with you,
give ourselves to and for our neighbor.
In hope, we pray, Amen.

PRAYER FOR UNCERTAIN TIMES

REV. NANCY LYNNE WESTFIELD, PhD
DREW UNIVERSITY THEOLOGICAL SCHOOL

Come, Holy Spirit,

The brokenness of our world makes us anxious, vulnerable, even distraught. Random acts of extremism strip the innocence from our children and draw tight the heartstrings of our community. The hard-won victories of our grandparents feel as if they are slipping toward defeat. We find ourselves buckling under the weight of ever-shifting but never-changing systemic oppressions and terror. We disconnect ourselves from those neighbors who are under siege and who are hunted—we prefer to be distant observers, numb to their pain. O Holy Spirit, comfort us. Be with us in this time of confusion and uncertainty. Soothe our restlessness and calm our fears. Help us resist the seduction of domination and the allure of violence. Sustain us, Holy Spirit—loose your passion for justice.

Even in our trouble, we are not content with simply making shallow remarks about the inequity of our world. Grant us the freedom to act in the confidence that God will bless our efforts. We yield to You so that every aspect of our lives would be infused with hope, conviction, and prophetic urgency. Holy Spirit, give us moral courage. Use us for Your purposes. Make us aware of Your presence, power, and glory. We call upon You to transform our fragile words into mighty deeds of liberation, care, and love for the sake of the Kin-dom. Grant us Your anointing—as only You can. Come, Holy Spirit, Your people cry out for You. Invade us! Meddle in our business! Occupy our wake, our sleep, our very souls! May we know that what God has hoped becomes a new reality. Amen.

Think about It. Talk about It.

What barriers or resistance do you see to the work of racial justice in your own life? In the life of your community?

What do you need to stop doing, or start doing, to have effective constructive conversations about race?

Engage

1. Using the two lists provided by John P. Kotter and Michael Beer, conduct an assessment of your church's or community's readiness to pay the price for uniting against racism. Ask the following:
   - Where can we improve in our commitment to act against racism?
   - What inhibits us from acting?
   - What could we, as a church or organization, do to support our growth in this area?
   - What can and will we draw upon to change?
2. Develop a "good neighbor policy" that expresses your (individual or church's) values and provides guidelines for relating to people of other races. Challenge yourself or your church to be proactive and take initiative rather than wait for others to show up.

Go Deeper. Read More.

Conger, Jay A., Gretchen M. Spreitzer, and Edward E. Lawler III, eds. *The Leader's Change Handbook: An Essential Guide to Setting Direction and Taking Action.* San Francisco: Jossey-Bass, 1999.

Horsman, Reginald. *Race and Manifest Destiny: The Origins of American Racial Anglo-Saxonism.* Cambridge, MA: Harvard University Press, 1981.

Forgiveness

He said to them, "When you pray, say: 'Father, hallowed be your name. Your kingdom come. Give us each day our daily bread. And forgive us our sins, for we ourselves forgive everyone indebted to us. And do not bring us to the time of trial.'"

—Luke 11:2–4

Key Terms

ETHICAL LONELINESS is "an experience of having been abandoned by humanity, compounded by the experience of not being heard. Such loneliness is a form of social abandonment that can be imposed only by multiple ethical lapses on the part of human beings residing in the surrounding world."[1]

FORGIVENESS is the act of canceling a penalty caused by an offender, of nullifying a wrongdoing. Forgiving one's self (the releasing of guilt and expectations of perfectionism), extending forgiveness to others, and accepting God's forgiveness are three sides of forgiveness.

KAIROS is a Greek term that refers to the right time, season, or opportunity for the accomplishment of a crucial action.

RETRIBUTION refers to the dispensing and receiving of compensation for harm or wrongs, especially for evil.

There can be no forgiveness without repentance, and there can be no repentance without retribution. But forgiveness demands that

---

1   Jill Stauffer, introduction to *Ethical Loneliness: The Injustice of Not Being Heard* (New York: Columbia University Press, 2015).

through God's power the sinner begins to live in the new cre-
ation, contributing positively for the welfare of the people of
God.

—J. N. K. Mugambi, *African Christian Theology*

Racial pain in our society today reflects historic and present structural injustice and ongoing injury. Racial pain is inflicted by outward expressions of harm, prejudice, and discrimination that can be documented. It is afflicted also by the complicity of silence that overlooks or ignores acts of injustice—unfairness—when they occur. While some people see this as "unethical loneliness," Jill Stauffer refers to the experience of "ethical loneliness," of being both abandoned and unheard:

> Ethical loneliness is the isolation one feels when one, as a vio-
> lated person or as one member of a persecuted group, has been
> abandoned by humanity, or by those who have power over one's
> life possibilities. It is a condition undergone by persons who
> have been unjustly treated and dehumanized by human beings
> and political structures, who emerge from that injustice only
> to find that the surrounding world will not listen to or can-
> not properly hear their testimony—their claims about what
> they suffered and about what is now owed them—on their own
> terms. . . . So ethical loneliness is the experience of having been
> abandoned by humanity compounded by the experience of not
> being heard.[2]

What do justice-seeking Christians need to overcome the ravages of racism? Is it possible to talk about forgiveness at all to people who have experienced abandonment? If so, who needs to forgive, and who needs to be forgiven? What does one do when grievous harm has been inflicted but the offender denies that any injury has occurred? And when injury is inflicted repeatedly?

---

2   Stauffer, *Ethical Loneliness.*

FORGIVENESS

I wrote this book because I believe truth-telling about America's original sin of racism must not be left to people of color alone. Crossing the bridge to a new America will be a multiracial task and vocation.

—Jim Wallis, *America's Original Sin*

Forgiveness is initially God's business. We all stand before God in universal need of grace, forgiveness, and restoration. God's grace flows freely in response to our need. When we reach for it, it is already there, preceding our request. In the parable of the prodigal son, the father runs to embrace the son with forgiveness the moment the son comes into the father's sight. When we come to God in all of our brokenness and inadequacy, God's response is acceptance and restoration. The state of being forgiven requires a reasoned response, a commitment to holy love and godly justice toward one's neighbors.

We seek to live God's Word. We will go forward from here forgiving, but also leading and demanding that the nation act on race.

—African Methodist Episcopal Church statement

What Archbishop Desmond Tutu said in his address about the ecumenical movement can also apply to the need for forgiveness between and among the races in America: "Our Lord prayed solemnly for the unity of His followers because the credibility of His own mission depended on it. Hence it cannot be a matter of indifference for Christians, this issue of the reunion of Christians. We have no option but to work and pray that we might all be one."[3]

Forgiveness is needed because unity cannot exist isolated from justice. And confession and repentance are required for forgiveness to work—to be efficacious. The call to holy living should therefore convict the hearts of white Christians in their strivings to embody an authentic

---

3   Desmond Tutu, "Towards Koinonia in Faith, Life and Witness," in *Fifth World Conference on Faith and Order*, ed. Thomas F. Best and Günther Gassmann (Geneva: World Council of Churches, 1994), 93–94.

Christianity for an inclusive, beloved community. Such efforts will include confession for participation in white privilege, repentance for perpetuation of ethical loneliness, and admission and expression of godly sorrow for complicity in the racial inequities of society and one's own racist actions as an individual.

> *The practice of forgiveness is not only, or even primarily, a way of dealing with guilt. Instead, its central goal is to reconcile, to restore communion—with God, with one another, and with the whole creation.*
> —L. Gregory Jones, *Practicing Our Faith,* by Dorothy C. Bass

In addressing injustices rooted in race, whites can be too eager to jump to talk about forgiveness rather than share some personal need and responsibility to repent, confess, and make concrete efforts to change, such as apology or reparations. Elizabeth Spelman reminds us that "just because something is broken or damaged doesn't mean it should be fixed or that anyone or everyone is entitled to fix it."[4]

Forgiveness of persons who commit, omit, or are complicit in acts of racism is necessary but insufficient alone. The journey to restoration must include white confession that calls for both individual and collective repentance and accountability. Repentance really begins when one starts to see the full dimensions of racism today: how the heinous, multiheaded monster of racism is deeply rooted in the history of this nation (see "Testimonies of Faith") and how that legacy has grown into a society within which racism is so engrained and accepted that those who live and work in positions of privilege and power can hardly see or recognize the ways racism is embedded in the political, economic, and cultural landscape. The great moral sins of the past have created a present society where it is impossible for whites even to opt out of the benefits of white privilege. The

---

4   Elizabeth V. Spelman, *Repair: The Impulse to Restore in a Fragile World* (Boston: Beacon, 2002).

white person's prayer for forgiveness from God must begin with this confession and repentance. Receiving God's forgiveness then fuels the conviction and change of heart to participate in God's work for transformation and justice.

White Americans sometimes question whether it is possible for a person or a group to repent for the evils that one's ancestors inflicted upon other peoples' ancestors, such as slavery in America. The heirs of this legacy can and should acknowledge the evils of the past and commit to making amends for the sins of their forebears. All who reap the ongoing benefits of those generations of slave labor are descendants, whether their genetic ancestors participated directly in the slave trade or not. The heirs now have a stark choice: whether to let injustice continue or not. In their book *No Innocent Bystanders*, coauthors Shannon Craigo-Snell and Christopher Doucot challenge whites to become allies for justice. They call white Christians to repent of the sin of racism by acknowledging the structural injustice of society and to move toward God by taking action against that injustice.[5] Indifference is itself complicity with a racist status quo. People who work as allies of justice demonstrate authentic Christianity.

People of color have borne—and continue to bear—the ongoing injury, injustice, and discrimination of racism. Moral outrage is both appropriate and ethically necessary. "Anger and resentment," philosopher Jill Stauffer says, "express a person's righteous indignation at being treated unjustly."[6] Righteous, holy anger can be powerful fuel for truth-telling and the search for justice. Jesus's words that we should forgive "seventy times seven"[7] have often been misused to justify continued oppression or abuse. Talk of forgiveness may seem meaningless in the face of the dominant group's refusal to recognize the complicity and denial of their own participation in the system itself.

---

5   Shannon Craigo-Snell and Christopher J. Doucot, *No Innocent Bystanders: Becoming an Ally in the Struggle for Justice* (Louisville, KY: Westminster John Knox, 2017), 62–63.

6   Stauffer, *Ethical Loneliness*, 8.

7   Matt. 18:22.

Forgiveness is vast—there really is no rational *reason for it. Justice by itself asks not for forgiveness but for restitution. Forgiveness requires some* great love, *a love that beckons one to another horizon, another place, another relationship. Sometimes this call is clear, and sometimes it lurks in the dark, is muffled, and requires faith even to catch a faint echo of its presence.*
                    —Matthew Fox, *Sins of the Spirit, Blessings of the Flesh*

Should we expect a people who have been harmed as a group by systemic racial injustice to carry the full weight and responsibility of forgiveness? Should they be looked to for initiating forgiveness toward a society that has, by commission or complicity, caused harm or injury to them through actions that continue to perpetuate racism, injustice, and inequality? Answering these questions is very likely to be related to our personal and race group history. The injured may be interested only in seeking to come to terms with what has happened without desiring any form of restored relationship with individuals who have directly inflicted harm on them.[8] People of color may not be interested in discussions of forgiveness given the persistence of ongoing discrimination and racial injustice.

South African Anglican Archbishop Desmond Tutu's "Prayer before Praying" from *The Book of Forgiving* describes the spiritual journey of forgiveness:

> *I am not yet ready for the journey*
> *I am not yet interested in the path*
> *I am at the prayer before the prayer of forgiveness*
> *Grant me the will to want to forgive*
> *Grant it to me not yet but soon . . .*[9]

---

8   Stauffer, *Ethical Loneliness*, 8.
9   Desmond M. Tutu and Mpho A. Tutu, *The Book of Forgiving: The Fourfold Path for Healing Ourselves and Our World* (New York: HarperOne, 2014), 9.

No one has the right to demand that someone else forgive: "Nothing here implies that it is the work of those who have been oppressed to forgive those who have benefited from their oppression."[10] The timetable of forgiveness—its timeliness, delay, or absence—is according to the movement of the Holy Spirit within one's heart. Those who have been wronged get to choose whether to forgive or to withhold forgiveness. Yet we affirm that forgiveness is part of authentic Christianity. Forgiveness is, ultimately, God's business: a gift of grace that comes in God's *kairos* moment, when and only when the time is right. Repentance, confession, and forgiveness are our business too.

PRAYER OF LAMENT FOR WHITE PEOPLE OF FAITH[11]

PAULA CLAYTON DEMPSEY
ALLIANCE OF BAPTISTS IN THE USA

How long, YHWH, how long will white people live in denial?

How long will we live insulated in racial comfort, ignoring the cries of our siblings of color for full inclusion, freedom, and justice?

How long, YWHW, how long will white people remain oblivious to our skin disease?

How long must our siblings of color bear pain in their souls because of our unwillingness to acknowledge the advantages gained through the disadvantages people of color experience?

How long will white people live lives of ease, protected from race-based stress and vulnerability because we are white while others suffer?

Awaken white people, O God of all people, to the damage and suffering caused when we fail to see "whiteness" as a racial identity.

---

10   Craigo-Snell and Doucot, *No Innocent Bystanders*, 66.
11   A Psalm prayer based on Psalm 13.

Awaken us to the reality that racism affects us all, and when we deny that fact, evil has prevailed.

O God of all, we acknowledge our spiritual wounds and the wounds of our ancestors that are the result of white supremacy.

Today we commit to the difficult work of examining, repairing, restoring, and reconciling relationships and institutions that have been marred for centuries by white privilege and supremacy.

How long? we ask. How long must we do this work?

Until all persons are respected, embraced, and affirmed as welcomed members of the family of God.

CONFESSING AND REPENTING WRONG

RUSSELL L. MEYER
FLORIDA COUNCIL OF CHURCHES

God of all, whose impartiality for love and grace is communicated to everyone in creation through the redemption made available in Christ Jesus, we come before you confessing our wrong and desiring our own repentance. Our European forefathers set out for fame and fortune under the banner of your church, claiming lands of indigenous peoples and enslaving those of darker pigmented skin. Their brutality was inexcusable, and yet too many in your church made excuses for it. Their violent conquest and taking of indigenous homelands was merciless, yet you are merciful. The contradiction did not phase the conquerors. They convinced themselves by skewing your Word that they were superior in human form and destined to be master of inferior races. They wrongly believed that Christianizing peoples required supplanting native culture and spiritualities with European habits and beliefs. Untold millions of our human brothers and sisters died because of European pride and self-righteousness. Native species and habitats were destroyed with abandon because Europeans and their descendants lacked respect for the ecosystems you had established over millennia. In the name of your Son Jesus, European ancestors killed, destroyed, and enslaved those they considered different from themselves.

Yet Jesus inaugurated his ministry in Nazareth, reading from Isaiah, "The Spirit of the Lord is upon me, because he has anointed me to bring good news to the poor. He has sent me to proclaim release to the captives and recovery of sight to the blind, to let the oppressed go free, to proclaim the year of the Lord's favor."[12]

He then said, "Today this scripture has been fulfilled in your hearing."[13] As he departed from the disciples, he instructed them, saying, "All authority in heaven and on earth has been given to me. Go therefore and make disciples of all nations, baptizing them in the name of the Father and of the Son and of the Holy Spirit, and teaching them to obey everything that I have commanded you."[14]

Forgive us, Gracious God, for twisting your Word to the benefit of the privileged and powerful, for betraying your Son before the peoples of the world, and for desecrating your creation with impunity. Break open our hearts so that we find among those who have been wronged new insight for living in just relationship with them and all creatures. Open our hands to make reparations so a future of trusting accompaniment is established. Open our wills to seek wisdom in all traditions, tossing our crowns at the feet of the cross of your Son, so that we might hear the wonders of redemption among people and within cultures we do not know. Turn us around so that we discover in others the majesty and mystery of your name that we have not known before among our own kind.

All peoples "live and move and have their being"[15] in you, for there is only "one God and Father of all, who is above all and through all and in all."[16] You are God, our God, and we plead for your mercy and the power of your Spirit to be renewed in inner knowledge and built up

12   Luke 4:18–19.
13   Luke 4:22.
14   Matt. 28:18–20.
15   Acts 17:28.
16   Eph. 4:6.

in true fellowship so that we become the fulfillment of the prayer of Jesus, your beloved anointed one: "That they may become completely one, so that the world may know that you have sent me and have loved them even as you have loved me."[17] In mercy, we pray. Amen.

Prepare Us, Lord . . .

Rev. Albert Starr Jr.
Director, Ethnic Specific and Multicultural Ministries
Program Director, African Descent Ministries
Evangelical Lutheran Church in America

What agreement has the temple of God with idols? For we are the temple of the living God; as God said, "I will live in them and walk among them, and I will be their God, and they shall be my people."[18]

You who created us out of the union of Your holy will and matchless power, You who breathed us into existence by the grace of Your loving kindness. Your very essence is love. You whose very nature is compassion. You brought forth humankind for relationship. We walk in this world guided by Your holy will to reflect the light, love, and power that You are. We come to you, God Most High.

Forgive us, Creator God, for surely we suffer in the cruel shadow of idols and illusions of supremacy. Some blindly robed in vanity and lies, some kept in tattered garments of fear, seduced to deny the equality of a person, You designed for us all to wear a nobler garment as Your creation.

Forgive us, Creator God, where we have bowed too quickly, too much, and too often to the lie that would exalt itself to sit upon a throne that belongs only to You. Only You are supreme, only You are the Almighty, only You are God Most High.

---

17   John 17:23.
18   2 Cor. 6:16.

Forgive us for being afraid. Call us out of the shadow of lies. Heal us in the light of Your holy truth. You know our brokenness. You know the torment that steals human souls and chains hearts You have fashioned for freedom. You know the enemy that would utterly devour us were it not for You.

Forgive us, God of Wonder. In Your forgiveness, there is redemption. In Your forgiveness, there is hope. In Your forgiveness, there is restoration.

Restore us in our knowing that You "break the cruel oppressor's rod." Restore us in knowing that Your rod, Your staff, is our shelter, our comfort, and our sanctuary. Restore us in our knowing, unite us in our knowing that You, who created us for Your divine purpose, have not abandoned us to the vile notions and schemes of racist hearts and minds.

Prepare us to serve Your will for justice in the face of empires, systems structures that raise up false authorities, diminishing the value of any human life on the false altar of racism, racial inferiority, or racial supremacy. Prepare us, Creator, to live to reflect Your Grace. Amen.

Think about It. Talk about It.

What are your thoughts about our individual and collective obligations to forgive?

Does the church (or society) share any responsibility today for past actions of America? How so?

How might acts of confession and repentance provide a suitable context for forgiveness to be reasonably considered and expressed?

What stands in the way of your church or community organization in doing the work of forgiveness for America's racial wrongdoings?

How would you talk about forgiveness in cases where you were the group or person experiencing the injustices?

Engage

1. Sponsor a listening tour. Ask and welcome black Americans to lead the tour as local informants. Set aside time to walk through the neighborhood of people of color to hear their stories, in their

space, through their eyes and experiences. Then reflect on and make notes about what you truly seek forgiveness for.

2. In your reading or study group, use the prayer of the psalmist (Psalm 51) to develop a prayer of confession informed by racial injustices in America and specific injustices and inequalities that exist in your community. Be as concrete as possible to name the "sins" for which confession is made. Use current, local news accounts to help your team develop your prayer. Consider using the prayer in an upcoming worship experience.

3. Develop plans that your community can and will implement to address one community racial disparity or injustice. Use John Kotter's eight steps ("The Price of Justice and Its Cost to Us") as a guide for the development of your work.

Go Deeper. Read More.

Donahue, J. R. *What Does the Lord Require: A Bibliographic Essay on the Bible and Social Justice.* St. Louis, MO: Institute of Jesuit Sources, 2000.

Harvey, Jennifer. *Dear White Christians: For Those Still Longing for Racial Reconciliation.* Grand Rapids, MI: William B. Eerdmans, 2014.

What Is the
Church to Do?

He has told you, O mortal, what is good;
and what does the Lord require of you
but to do justice, and to love kindness,
and to walk humbly with your God?

—Micah 6:8

Key Terms

AGAPĒ is a Greek term for a type of love commonly expressed in religious contexts. It connotes charity, devotion, esteem, or respect. *Agapē* is frequently associated with one of the most important terms of the Hebrew scriptures, *hesed.*

BELOVED COMMUNITY is a term that informed Martin Luther King Jr.'s vision and prophetic ministry. It is akin to the ideal state for which Jesus prays in John 17.

So, the Church must cry out for justice, and thereby resist the cynicism fueled by visions that failed and dreams that died. The Church must insist on justice, and thereby refuse to blame victimized people for their situations. The Church must insist on justice, and thereby assure participation of all people.
      —Evangelical Lutheran Church in America statement

In his "Letter from a Birmingham Jail," Martin Luther King Jr. wrote, "Injustice anywhere is a threat to justice everywhere. We are caught in an inescapable network of mutuality, tied in a single garment of destiny. Whatever affects one directly, affects all indirectly."[1] This often quoted statement is rooted in Martin Luther King Jr.'s vision of a beloved community. A key to understanding the transformative character of a beloved community is the dynamic principle of transcendence. A beloved community continuously works toward the dismantling of all barriers—racism, sexism, classism, nationalism, militarism, and others—that negate unity and community from realization.

White individuals and church communities can demonstrate repentance for the ongoing racial injustices in society in several concrete ways. They can share the laments of people of color. Churches of all races can identify white supremacy when and where it presents itself and as a sin against God and neighbor. Churches can join together to reverse the injustices inherent in and as a result of white privilege. They can unite and participate in discussions and actions on restitution and reparations. Such actions, to be transformative of "America's original sin," must focus on confronting and demolishing every obstacle that stifles, hinders, or inhibits individuals and groups from embodying our collective humanity. There can be no community without unity, without giving attention to our "inescapable network of mutuality."

Rahab displayed *hesed* as she chose to offer kindness to Israelite spies whom she did not know.[2] Apostle Paul writes a similar word as he corrects the behaviors of the churches of Galatia, who sought to erect standards and barriers that resulted in divisions in the community. He writes, "For in Christ Jesus neither circumcision nor uncircumcision counts for anything; the only thing that counts is faith working through love."[3] Jesus expresses this kind, merciful, self-giving love in the last words of his final prayer in the Gospel according to John: "I made your name known, so that the love with which you have loved me may be in them, and I in them."[4]

---

1 Martin Luther King Jr., "Letter from a Birmingham Jail," April 16, 1963, https://www.africa.upenn.edu/Articles_Gen/Letter_Birmingham.html.
2 Josh. 2:12.
3 Gal. 5:6.
4 John 17:26.

Agapē, like *hesed*, acts to overcome barriers of gender, ethnic origin, culture, and social status because of its intrinsic character. This is the foundation of an authentic Christianity in which people strive to become an inclusive, beloved community. Such love balances the scales for people and groups to live in right relationship. In an inclusive, beloved community, justice is operative, where fairness for the powerful works equally on behalf of the powerless. The biblical mandate that "you and the alien who resides with you shall have the same law and the same ordinance"[5] means that there is no dual standard. It is a demand for equal justice, equal treatment, equal participation, equal opportunity, and equal honor for everyone. It rejects institutional injustice for the disempowered.

> *From the beginning of human existence, justice has been a key element in God's revelation for human relationships. The Old Testament Prophets' words of condemnation and the need for repentance as well as their vision of the Kingdom of God, emphasize that peace and full life come from Justice. As churches of Jesus Christ, we acknowledge that we have not always shown leadership in issues of justice. At this time, God is calling us more strongly than ever to take a prophetic stance and move from powerful rhetoric to critical action. The call is to raise the banner against racial injustice and to make a significant impact on our nation and throughout the world.*
> —National Council of Churches of Christ in the USA

In a nation where people of color do not receive equal justice, an authentic Christianity that seeks to unfold into an inclusive, beloved community calls us to righteousness. Christian advocacy must be in solidarity with those experiencing oppression. Jim Wallis suggests a person-to-person multifaceted approach:

---

5   Num. 15:16.

1. to have "focused, honest, serious, and disciplined conversations on race between white people and people of color" and to believe each other's experiences;
2. to change the "geography" of racial segregation by one's own choices in where you live and whom you befriend;
3. to have "a new conversation on race" in our daily lives, such as in schools, sports, and churches.[6]

Predominantly white churches are implicated in racial injustice. Each church's and denomination's history is different, and their stories vary depending on their tradition and locale. Yet their ongoing participation in structures of white privilege forms an ecumenism of complicity. Bearing and confessing their corporate guilt is an expression of the Catholicity (universality) of the faith. Insisting that the time has come, the World Council of Churches is calling on faith communities to be "agents of transformative justice in the face of racial injustice."[7] Talk is cheap if the churches do not also engage in activities and advocacy with conviction and determination to dismantle racism at every level: local, regional, national, and international. The churches and the ecumenical community must work together against injustice, prejudice, and bigotry. Authentic Christianity is an agent of love. Churches must support the maintenance of moral integrity. Churches must change. Churches must lead in making appropriate restitution for wrongdoings and take corrective action so that old, harmful practices and policies end. Churches must claim, embrace, and embody the values and standards of Jesus—doing no harm, protecting the least and the vulnerable, and setting free the oppressed to become God's inclusive, beloved community.

---

6   These three points are relevant to the current work. For a full discussion, see Jim Wallis, *America's Original Sin: Racism, White Privilege, and the Bridge to a New America* (Grand Rapids, MI: Brazos, 2016), 195–219.

7   World Council of Churches, "The Work of Truth-Telling Has to Happen" (press release, September 28, 2017), http://www.oikoumene.org/en/press-centre/news/the -work-of-truth-telling-has-to-happen.

The church can and must be an agent to bring about restorative justice and be an agent for change. Congregations and denominations across America are taking action to express an authentic Christianity, which moves toward an inclusive, beloved community. Such activities will express God's refreshing, renewing, and redeeming love at work, healing divisions caused by racism, promoting justice, reconciling broken relationships, and repairing communities that we might become "one nation under God with liberty and justice for all."

The Episcopal Church has identified racial reconciliation as a priority, seeking to "1) tell the truth about church and race; 2) rewrite the narrative; 3) form Episcopalians as reconcilers; 4) repair and restore institutions and society."[8] Since 1998, the Christian Church (Disciples of Christ) has made antiracism/pro-reconciliation a major denominational priority, creating reconciliation ministries to target racism as "a spiritual and theological dilemma as well as a social evil."[9] There are many other churches and denominations working to address racism and to strive for racial justice and the promotion of a beloved community.

But seek the welfare of the city where I have sent you into exile, and pray to the Lord on its behalf, for in its welfare you will find your welfare.[10]

In 2007, President Jimmy Carter invited church leaders from every area of the nation to gather for the purpose of mending the theological and racial divides of Christians belonging to more than thirty Baptist traditions, organizations, and associations. From his call, the New Baptist Covenant was formed. Using Covenants of Action as a facilitating tool, two or more churches commit to work beyond barriers of racial segregation

---

8   The Episcopal Church, "The Jesus Movement," 2017, https://www.episcopalchurch
      .org/jesus-movement.
9   Christian Church (Disciples of Christ), "The Initiative: Many Members, One Table,"
      Reconciliation Ministry, 1998, http://reconciliationministry.org/who-we-are/the
      -initiative/.
10   Jer. 29:7.

and theological disputes to "engage in serious and hard conversations about what it means to form a covenant with each other."[11] For example, Ebenezer Baptist Church, Greater Piney Grove Baptist Church, and Park Avenue Baptist Church of Atlanta, Georgia, united to address childhood illiteracy, while Wilshire Baptist Church and Friendship-West Baptist Church joined to combat predatory lending in their neighborhood.

We need to find or create venues for conversation, places where stories of lament and pain, healing and hope are told, heard, and honored in openness and in safety. The National Museum of African American History and Culture in Washington, DC, and the National Civil Rights Museum in Memphis are such venues. In Providence, Rhode Island, the closed Cathedral of St. John has been transformed into the Center for Reconciliation, with a mission to address the ongoing consequences of slavery and to work for social justice and racial reconciliation. The African American Methodist Heritage Center for the United Methodist Church, the African American Episcopal Historical Collection of the Virginia Theological Seminary and the Historical Society of the Episcopal Church document the contributions of black Americans in those denominational contexts. These collaborations are personal, relational, institutional, and systemic.

PRAYER OF REMINDER AND TURNING

L. CALLID KEEFE-PERRY
THE RELIGIOUS SOCIETY OF FRIENDS (QUAKERS)

O Holy Power,

We labor under the weight of the knowledge that our systems and structures
are built on the backs of those who have struggled most.

---

11   http://newbaptistcovenant.org/our-calling-new/.

We know and name that those very same systems and structures
remain pressing down
on the shoulders and souls of those who still toil the most.
And so today, God, we ask that you soften our hearts,
bend down our necks, and give us sight.

To those of us with power who believe we have done all that we
can, grant a reminder of humility. Allow us to see how our words and
solidarity are but shadows of the family we can be—of the family we
already are in your sight. We ask for the evil in us to be weakened and
the good raised up.

To those of us who suffer under power and turn at times to despair,
grant a reminder that there is strength to resist. Allow us to see that
there are moments every day in which we can push back and press on
with a fierce love. We ask to know a full measure of Grace, experiencing that compassion and encouragement in the flesh.

To those who struggle daily to seek out some way when there seems
to be none, grant that we find one another, are humble as needed, and
are bold when required. Allow us to know one another in that which
is eternal, to strengthen one another, and to lift one another up with
tenderness. We ask for the courage to use our lives in service to the
dismantling of white supremacy and wickedness in high places and to
the building up of that which we find in your peaceable reign.

In all days, keep us from idols, from thinking *our* way is *the* way
and that our path is the most holy. We know we will be tempted to
think ourselves better than others, and so we ask to remember that
the steps needed only end in you. What we call "good" now is only a
glimmer of what can be built and is to come in Christ. We say "justice"
but know little of its depth. We say "equality" but struggle to see how
much needs to change. We are like thieves; we take good words for our
use and for our pride, but we know little of what they can be.

God, give us an opening to change,
turn us from our idols of politeness and properness,

guide us from certainty to confession,
and in that space, convict us and bring us through.
We are yours in service on this day and for all days.
And so we pray that we might have the courage to serve.

Amen.

Little children, keep yourselves from idols.[12]

A Prayer for Parents Everywhere

CHARLES R. FOSTER
CANDLER SCHOOL OF THEOLOGY
EMORY UNIVERSITY

This prayer was inspired by a photograph of a black American mother and father engaged in an intense conversation with their ten- to twelve-year-old son. In the background is a television split-screen picture with a white policeman on one side and a black American man on the other. It brought to mind parents everywhere struggling to name for their children dangerous situations they will face, to explain threatening circumstances they will encounter, to prepare them to recognize the appeals of evil in its many forms.

We offer this prayer consequently for parents struggling to find words to prepare their children for

- any form of discrimination they may experience—racism, sexism, homophobia, or prejudice against individuals with different abilities;
- the excessive and unwanted attention of an adult family member, teacher, or scout leader;

---

12   1 John 5:21.

- the aggression of a bully;
- a life-threatening illness;
- the loss of a family member, job, or home.

This prayer is also offered for parents who try to explain to their children

- why bombs are dropping on their city,
- why their school went into lockdown mode,
- why there is not enough food to satisfy their hunger,
- why a loved one is going to prison.

O God of mercy and grace,
   justice and peace,
   love and hope,
we pray for your compassionate and healing presence
in the difficult conversations of parents,
   foster parents, and grandparents,
   here and everywhere with their children.
We pray they will discover the persistence of your grace
as they seek to explain the unexplainable.
Strengthen their resolve when they see no justice.
Be present when they feel alone.
Provide safety where they find no peace.
Uphold them when they must be strong.
Make them bold when their children need protection.
Help them speak wisely to thwart words of hate and discrimination.
Help them love unconditionally to undermine prejudice and bias.
Help them see alternative possibilities when none seem evident.
Help them discover that in these difficult moments, they are not alone,
   for you, O God, are with them.

   Amen.

A Corporate Prayer

Sharon Watkins
Christian Church (Disciples of Christ)

God of justice and righteousness and peace,
You who have promised to be with us always,
We open ourselves to your presence in this hour.

Even as our hearts break over violent and senseless death, over a devastated planetary home, over greed that outweighs human need, over the church's too frequent complicity in racism and the resulting trauma to too many of your children, we know that you, also, are anguished.

And yet, you do not abandon us. Instead you call us forth and equip us for resilience, resistance, and persistence in your name. You inspire us with a vision of creation living in wholeness, and you breathe into us energy and commitment to work to and witness the fulfillment of that vision.

We are grateful.

And so, O God, as the sea roars and the desert lifts up its voice in praise, as wind and leaves and rain declare your glory, help us join the chorus, offering holy hallelujahs for the life, the love, the hope that comes from you.

Bless each one of us, we pray, all who gather here, that we may hear your call and follow.

In Jesus's name,
Amen.

PRAYER FOR HEALING

JOHN DORHAUER
UNITED CHURCH OF CHRIST

We pray, God of all, for the healing of our nation.

In opposition to your will for human community and in violation of your vision for a world of shalom, this nation was born in the cauldron of racial division.

For more than four hundred years, a single race has maintained the right to own, enslave, degrade, oppress, and humiliate all other races.

One race alone has assumed the right, in your name, to call itself superior.

One race alone has accumulated power and wealth with little regard for what that has done to all other races within this land.

We are in deep need of your power to transform lives.

We are a nation that has healed the wounds of its people lightly—often crying, "Peace, peace" when there is no peace.

Neither our Civil War nor our civil rights movement has ended race hate. We remain a deeply divided people. We have not chosen a pathway to the kind of redress and reparations that would atone for past sins and create racial equity.

Let all who call your name remain faithful to your vision of Shalom.

Let all who worship you fulfill their covenant promise to do your will.

Let all who are inspired by your grace become agents of your justice.

May there arise within the heart of all your disciples a collective will to confront the principalities and powers that build barriers of exclusion instead of bridges for inclusion. With Jesus as our guide, let us not count the cost of such discipleship. Let us run with perseverance this race set before us.

Stir within us all a passion for race equity. Let no one's skin color determine their status. Let no one's skin color limit or enhance their ability to pursue happiness. Let no one's skin color affect how another perceives their worth. Let every black mother's child grow into adulthood without the threat of their rights being negotiated by a white person with both the will and the ability to do so. Call America to become the land we once dreamed of: a land where all are created equal. Amen.

A PRAYER BASED ON THE BELHAR CONFESSION

REV. SHELDON W. SORGE, PhD
GENERAL MINISTER
PRESBYTERY OF PITTSBURGH, PRESBYTERIAN CHURCH (USA)

This prayer is based on a church confession from South Africa in the 1980s, adopted by the Presbyterian Church (USA) in 2016. It is one of twelve historic church confessions that the Presbyterian Church includes in its constitution. This prayer is suitable for use in worship as a confession of sin, or it can be used as an affirmation of faith by substituting the second person "you" with "God" and adjusting verbs accordingly. The full text of the Belhar Confession is available in *The Book of Confessions.*[13]

Holy God,
   We acknowledge that the unity of your church is both your gift and our obligation, both a binding force and something we must diligently seek. Our Lord Jesus prays for our unity yet leaves it to us to maintain the unity of the Spirit in the bonds of peace.
   We confess that we have spurned your gift of unity; we have broken the Spirit's bonds. We have permitted racial descent, along with other social factors, to determine who belongs and

---

13   *The Book of Confessions: The Constitution of the Presbyterian Church (U.S.A.) Part 1* (Louisville, KY: Presbyterian Church [USA], 2016), 285–97.

leads in our fellowship. In so doing, we have sinned against you, impoverished ourselves, violated our brothers and sisters, and diminished the credibility and effectiveness of your church in the world. In your mercy, forgive us.

We pray that your Spirit would so move upon us and among us that we would let nothing bar us from communion with anyone who has true faith in Jesus Christ. Stir up in us actions, not mere words, that reach out in direct connection with people whose ethnic heritage is different from our own. Make us into a city on a hill, a light to the world, a public demonstration of your reign in which all peoples are joined in full reconciliation. Rouse up our anger at all the ways racial discrimination persists both in the church and in the world, that we would no longer be conformed to the world but transformed by the renewing of our minds. Create in us a clean heart, and renew in us a right spirit.

We reject the prejudice, fear, selfishness, and unbelief that deny the reconciling power of the gospel. We embrace and honor all our brothers and sisters in Christ from every race and nation, and we resolve to be likewise peaceable to all persons regardless of creed. Unto you be all honor and glory in this world and in the world to come. In the name and for the sake of our Lord and Savior, Jesus Christ. Amen.

PRAYER FOR RACIAL JUSTICE

REV. MARGARET R. ROSE
PRESIDING BISHOP'S DEPUTY FOR ECUMENICAL
AND INTER-RELIGIOUS RELATIONS
THE EPISCOPAL CHURCH

Ever-Creating God,

In these times, it might be easier to despair. Each day's news offers ample reason.

Too often we see and experience the destruction of your world. The promise of abundant life for all is a distant vision.

Free us from passive acceptance of this news. Make us actors with you in seeking your justice and love.

Open our eyes to our complicity in unjust structures and racial inequity.

Open our eyes to the systems that deepen the gulfs among us.

Open our eyes to ways we wound the image of you in ourselves and neglect your image in one another.

Help us love each other, not only for what we have in common, but also for how we are different.

Help us see new ways of being and living in your world. Make us brave.

For you are a God of hope, who makes all things new, again and yet again!

You are the God who created us and the world and called it good.

Return us to your original blessing, where differences among us are occasions of celebration, beauty, and hope.

Transform us and give us courage to work toward abundance for all.

May these prayers be the expression of our public voice, a word to declare that we are not bound by this original sin of racism but by the blessing of a Creator whose love ever reforms us and sends us forth with power and hope for a world made new. Amen.

Think about It. Talk about It.

How do we as the church name racial injustice as sin and repent?

Where might you create spaces that bear prophetic witness in your community and in your church?

How do we as the church and as individuals commit ourselves to the struggle for racial justice?

Engage

Sponsor a citywide or area-wide reading challenge and conversation. In February 2017, the cities of Louisville, Kentucky, and Richmond,

Virginia, were challenged by concerned people of good will to read *The Color of Law: A Forgotten History of How Our Government Segregated America*.[14] In Louisville, as part of the Angela Project (named for the first enslaved person to set foot on American soil), a church hosted a free, live-streamed conversation about the book to learn and discuss the systemic character of racism.

Host a series of conversations on race relations and possible roles of churches in your community.

1. Identify and list race-related incidents written about in your local newspaper.
2. Ask people to discuss their "theory of the event." Who or what is the cause? Why? How do these things happen? Can they imagine viewing the incident from the life of the "other"?
3. Encourage them to share their feelings, hopes, frustrations, and fears.
4. Consider what the church can do that they are willing to help implement.

Go Deeper. Read More.
Davies, Susan, E. *Ending Racism in the Church*. Cleveland, OH: United Church Press, 1998.
"Race Relations." ThoughtCo. https://www.thoughtco.com/race-relations -4132982.
Rah, Soong-Chan. *The Next Evangelicalism: Freeing the Church from Western Cultural Captivity*. Downers Grove, IL: InterVarsity Press, 2009.

---

14 Richard Rothstein, *The Color of Law: A Forgotten History of How Our Government Segregated America* (New York: Liveright, 2017).

JUSTICE AND
SPIRITUAL PRACTICES

Yet, O LORD, you are our Father; we are the clay, and you are our
potter; we are all the work of your hand.

—Isaiah 64:8

Key Terms

EUCHARIST is one of several terms used to honor the final meal Jesus shared
with his closest followers. HOLY COMMUNION and the LORD'S SUPPER are terms
used by Christian religious traditions to refer to the same experience.

SOLIDARITY commonly refers to the coming together of people to further their
self-interest, but not necessarily at the expense of others.[1] A Christian
view of solidarity refers to the extension of one's self beyond one's self-
interests in service to others.

SPIRITUAL PRACTICE here is interchangeable with spiritual discipline. Christian
spiritual practices refer to the intentional, patterned, routine acts that
orient a person's relationship with God, with others, and with creation for
nurturing development of an authentic, integrated, and responsible self.

SPIRITUALITY may refer to the ways and means by which people relate to the
world that provide meaning, purpose, and direction for their lives.

Authentic spirituality wants to open us to truth—whatever truth
may be, wherever truth may take us. Such a spirituality does not
dictate where we must go, but trusts that any path walked with

---

1   David A. Hardcastle and Patricia R. Powers, *Community Practice: Theories and Skills for*
Social Workers 2nd ed. (New York: Oxford University Press, 2004), 130.

integrity will take us to a place of knowledge. Such a spirituality encourages us to welcome diversity and conflict, to tolerate ambiguity, and to embrace paradox. By this understanding, the spirituality of education is not about dictating ends. It is about examining and clarifying the inner sources of teaching and learning, ridding us of the toxins that poison our hearts and minds.

—Parker J. Palmer, The Promise of Paradox: A Celebration of Contradictions in the Christian Life

What are we being called to do for racial justice as individual Christians, as members of the Church of Christ, and as citizens of American society today? Taking up various spiritual practices may help answer the question. Discernment—practices that help reveal what is hidden, obscure, or concealed—is one set of actions that can help Christians and people of good will uncover what and how God calls us to respond to racism. We need to undertake a process of discernment, individually and collectively, to develop responses to these questions. Personal and communal prayers are spiritual practices encouraged throughout this book that will assist in awakening and responding to the causes and consequences of racism too. Justice is the work of our prayers.[2] The unity Jesus prayed for requires us to advocate for racial justice as we achieve the concord that existed between Jesus and God.[3] Undertaking spiritual practices, we believe, will help lead churches toward living out an authentic Christianity that is inclusive and affirming of a beloved community.

Participation in the sacraments or ordinances of the church is another set of spiritual practices that can help shape and pattern our lives for public proclamation of Christ's call to live a holy life, uniting us with Christians everywhere. In the Episcopal Church's liturgy of baptism, the vow is to "seek and serve Christ in all persons, loving your neighbor

---

2   Kaji Douska, "Building," in *Still Speaking Daily Devotions* (Cleveland, OH: United Church of Christ, 2018).

3   John 17:6–26.

as yourself," and to "strive for justice and peace among all people and respect the dignity of every human being."[4] The United Methodist Church asks of persons seeking baptism and membership in its body, "Do you accept the freedom and power God gives you to resist evil, injustice, and oppression in whatever form they present themselves?"[5] Other traditions may use different baptismal language, but the underlying Christian challenge is the same: there can be no bigotry or racial supremacy when we see each other with the eyes of Christ and seek to follow Christ's command to love our neighbors.

The liturgy of the Eucharist (reenactment of the Lord's Supper) brings our history and our now into God's eternal present for redemption, offering manna and hope for the journey. Our individual lives and our collective humanity are transformed and remembered by Christ's life, death, and resurrection. As we unite with Christ in Holy Communion, we are united with all creation and all peoples. That moment is a moment of sacred conviction, of judgment on human life smudged with sin and hatred and barriers and violence and hurt and division. We are given a vision of how our world could and should be radically different as the reign of God on earth.

In their book, *A Body Broken, a Body Betrayed: Race, Memory, and Eucharist in White-Dominant Churches*, Mary McClintock Fulkerson and Marcia W. Mount Shoop write, "Dangerous memory follows Jesus as the 'dangerous Christ' into solidarity with those who have been harmed by the powerful. Jesus' solidarity with the oppressed was and is about liberation from suffering and oppression. Jesus' ministry was about transformation."[6] Jesus expressed solidarity by his sacrifice, which was beyond self-interest to the point of death. Engagement with Jesus

---

4   The Episcopal Church, *The Book of Common Prayer* (New York: Church Publishing, 1979), 305.

5   The United Methodist Church, *The United Methodist Hymnal* (Nashville, TN: United Methodist Publishing House, 1989), 34.

6   Mary McClintock Fulkerson and Marcia W. Mount Shoop, *A Body Broken, a Body Betrayed: Race, Memory, and Eucharist in White-Dominant Churches* (Eugene, OR: Cascade Books, 2015), 66.

through the reenactment of his Last Supper impels us to live in Jesus's call for the transformation of our lives and our society. Participation in Holy Communion is a spiritual practice that can inform our work of justice.[7]

> *Loving one's enemies requires* grace—*an in-breaking of the long, long vision of a greater love, higher justice, and deeper acceptance beyond deserving. Compassion does not remove the rage or silence the outrage; it gives a prophetic voice of hope. The hope that justice, if not obtained for oneself, can be guaranteed for those who follow and that gives strength to continue the struggle, meaning to transform pain, courage even in suffering.*
> —David W. Augsburger, *Hate-Work: Working through the Pain and Pleasures of Hate*

As spiritual practices are able to inform our work for the rights and equalities of all, justice can also inform our spiritual practices. Much attention has been given to the ways spirituality informs justice understandings and actions. Awareness is also needed for justice to infuse and shape our spiritual practices and disciplines. John Powell writes, "Social justice and spirituality are . . . in a recursive relationship."[8] Why do we assume that enhanced spirituality flows in the direction of increased solidarity with people who are oppressed and marginalized? When justice informs spirituality, spirituality can help the person or group adjust to and make meaning of the situation or can motivate individuals or a group to transform the social arrangements that lead to racism, oppression, and marginalization. Doing what is fair in the face of harm and advocating for what is right in the presence of microaggressive acts of discrimination may enrich a person's spiritual orientation toward God

---

7 John A. Powell, *Racing to Justice: Transforming Our Conceptions of Self and Other to Build an Inclusive Society* (Bloomington: Indiana University Press, 2012), 197–228.
8 Powell, 197.

and enhance a group's sensitivities and compassion for the plight of persons and groups who are victimized by racism.[9]

Being and becoming an authentic Christian involves taking up spiritual disciplines. Working for justice can inform our spiritual practices. The work of justice and orienting ourselves to the way of Jesus require intentional practices of inclusion and love. Other habits, practices, and values to take up as we act now to end racism may include the following:

- providing protection and safety for the well-being of vulnerable persons in our nation and world
- encouraging the maintenance of moral integrity
- fostering the practice of honesty
- nurturing openness to engage in truth-telling as dialogue rather than one-way communication
- supporting individual and collective responsibility
- encouraging one another and communities to live lives of simplicity—that is, with unadulterated motives or nonduplicitous actions as a spiritual practice

These and other practices help build trust, the foundation for healthy relationships on the journey to end racism in the Church and our nation. The embodiments of these habits, practices, and values help us reclaim an authentic Christianity for the building of beloved communities.

A spirituality of justice has a common goal, a vision of harmony and health in relationships, a concern for equal opportunity and mutual privilege.
—David W. Augsburger, *Hate-Work: Working through the Pain and Pleasures of Hate*

Together in Christ, we are called to be agents of change, to break down barriers, to facilitate honest dialogue, and to build just communities.

---

9   Powell, 201–3.

Racial injustice diminishes us all. To preach reconciliation without the commitment "to struggle on the side of the oppressed for justice," warns theologian Walter Wink, is "nothing but thin air."[10] To treat each engagement with a person as an encounter with Christ himself is to recognize the image of God in everyone. As Mount Vernon United Methodist Church in Washington, DC, prays in its Litany of Remembrance and Repentance, let us all pray for "wisdom and courage to disrupt, dismantle and destroy racism of every form, public and private, spoken and silent."[11] God is calling all Christians and churches to join in the Holy Spirit's creative and redeeming work for racial justice wherever we serve.

PRAYER OF CONFESSION AND COMMITMENT

W. FRANKLYN RICHARDSON
SENIOR PASTOR
GRACE BAPTIST CHURCH

O God our Mother . . . and Father,
We thank you for being accessible to us! We acknowledge that we live beneath your divine intention, having been made in your divine image.

We have allowed our sin to distort who you made us to be, a sin that has fanned the flame of hate, grounded in discrimination, prejudice, and the superiority of one people over another, which devalues all humanity. This hate has been concretized in our institutions and systems and threatens to destroy us all, nationally and globally.

Lord, help us return to the vision you have for us, free of racism and all the -isms that paralyze us from becoming a beloved community.

---

10 Walter Wink, *When the Powers Fall: Reconciliation in the Healing of Nations* (Minneapolis, MN: Fortress, 1998), 26.
11 Donna Claycomb Sokol, "A Day to Remember and Repent," *Words from Washington* (blog), October 8, 2017, http://wordsfromwashington.blogspot.com/2017/10/a-day-to-remember-and-repent.html.

Give us the capacity to own whatever complicity we have in the distortion of your intention and the courage to be agents of change. Forgive us for our silence and our long delay to take action. As we commit ourselves to reflect the biblical mandate "to do justice, and to love mercy and to walk humbly before our God,"[12] give us fresh Christian faith to act out of a renewed commitment to Christ. Help us hear the gospel fresh and clearly. In Jesus's name, Amen.

BECOMING THE CHRISTIAN

NATHANIEL D. WEST
SAMUEL DEWITT PROCTOR SCHOOL OF THEOLOGY
VIRGINIA UNION UNIVERSITY

Most gracious and heavenly God, with a humble mind and contrite heart, I submit this prayer, acknowledging that at times, I have not lived up to the promise of glorifying You and edifying humanity. I admit that I have not always given to others the same love and kindness that You freely give to me.

Forgive me, God, for the negative judgment I have placed upon others simply based on the color of their skin. Forgive me, God, for creating and believing in stereotypes that diminish and demean others. Forgive me, God, for constructing discriminatory policies and participating in inequitable practices that have benefited me personally while simultaneously demeaning and degrading others. Free me from the traps of selfishness and individualism that cause me to discount, dismiss, and even disapprove of the cries, complaints, and concerns of others.

Lord, I not only seek Your forgiveness; I also ask for guidance. Lead and guide me in the right paths—the paths of justice, the paths of equity, the paths of truth, and the paths of righteousness—for the cause of Christ. Change me so I can be a voice for the voiceless, a healer

---

12   Mic. 6:8b.

and a helper, an advocate and an activist. Use me to make the crooked paths straight, to mend the brokenhearted, and to rebuild that which has been torn down.

God, I simply want to be and do that which I have been created for. Thank You for healing me, thank You for building me up, thank You for forgiving me, thank You for loving me, thank You for blessing me, and thank You for seeing me. Now, God, use me as an instrument of healing, an instrument of building, an instrument of forgiving, an instrument of loving, an instrument of blessing—so when people see me, they see You. Amen.

A PRAYER FOR PLACE-MAKING

RANDY G. LITCHFIELD
BROWNING PROFESSOR OF CHRISTIAN EDUCATION
METHODIST THEOLOGICAL SCHOOL IN OHIO

Our sustaining God, you are the great I Am, the Place[13] of all that is and all we are. In you, we find perfect love, justice, peace, and courage.

Our redeeming God, you are the great I Am, the Place of restarts. In you, our brokenness and our giftedness open to your purposes.

Our creating God, you are the great I AM, the PLACE of possibilities and hope. In you, the vision of the Kin-dom calls and claims us.

I Am . . . Place, through the ages, your emerging Kin-dom challenges the empire of this world. Freedom challenges slavery. Liberty challenges oppression. Giftedness challenges deprivation. Agency challenges addiction. Community challenges isolation. Compassion challenges dehumanization. Hope challenges despair. Shalom challenges violence. Life abundant challenges death.

---

13   In Jewish tradition, *Hammaqom* (the Place) is one of the circumlocutions the rabbis used as the name for God (John Kampen, professor in the Dunn Chair in Biblical Interpretation at Methodist Theological School in Ohio, private email correspondence, September 22, 2016).

Place-making God, make us fit partners in your reconciling and liberating work. Empower us to work with you as a people fashioning the places we dwell and the routes we travel in light of the Kin-dom. In our times, help us challenge empire in the form of racism.

May our prayers open us to your vision, provide discernment, and
ground us in your presence to empower us for facing racism.
May our reflections pierce self-deceptions, name systems, and foster
strategies that enable us to expose racism.
May our study of sacred texts and the saints remind us of your
faithfulness, form our imagination, and grant us courage to
declare racism in all its forms as sin.
May our formation of character create empathy, build solidarity
with others, and develop commitment to confront racism.
May our actions embody hope, offer redemption, and lead
to transformation that helps us end racism.

I Am . . . Place, make us place-makers, and may the places we make be
reflections of your Kin-dom. Amen.

PRAYER OF ACCOUNTABILITY

JANE SIEBERT
GENERAL CONVENTION OF THE SWEDENBORGIAN
CHURCH OF NORTH AMERICA

To You who listens to our hearts, knows us, loves us equally, and created us to live in harmony,
We say thank You.
We need Your help this day and forever more.
We need Your help to envision a world of racial equity,
where all have what they need for health, education, justice, and
family support,

for we must first be able to imagine it to make it so.

Help us all to want this and work for this with all our heart and all our
soul and all our might.

May it be so.

We need Your help to open our individual eyes to the part we each play
in our blindness to what is and what isn't.

Help us identify our own wrongs so we can work to make them right.

May it be so.

We need Your help to learn over and over how to love as You taught
us to love,

with open hearts, open minds, and open arms.

Help us see You in every person, hear You in every plea, feel You in
every possibility.

May it be so.

May this be our individual prayer as well as our collective prayer, for
it takes all of us,

every minute of every day, never looking away, always looking within.

Amen.

Think about It. Talk about It.

How do you define or describe your spirituality?

What spiritual practices inform your views of racial justice?

What acts of justice contribute to and challenge your understandings
of spirituality?

Where is the "dangerous Christ" calling you to go for the cause of
racial justice?

What is the "dangerous Christ" moving you to confrontation as a
response to racism?

What are your congregation's marks of an authentic Christianity?

Engage

1. Discernment. Invite your group or congregation to set aside regu-
    lar times for silence and prayer for openness to God's concern and
    vision for race relations.

2. Hospitality. As God is our refuge and strength,[14] churches must
    become communities that cultivate a gracious and caring com-
    munity. Ask persons to discuss when they do/do not experience
    hospitality or feel welcomed and places where they feel excluded.
    Develop a list of behaviors and actions that your group or com-
    munity will commit to uphold that promote justice for marginal-
    ized groups or fairness of racial equality.

3. Justice work. Doing justice is a central tenet of all three Abrahamic
    religious traditions—Judaism, Christianity, and Islam. Conduct a
    personal and communal assessment of the range of actions you/
    your group or church intentionally do to advocate for and support
    fair treatment of persons of other races. Challenge yourself/your
    group/your church to come up with ways you can do more to
    repair the fractures and remove the barriers of racism.

Go Deeper. Read More.

Morris, R. C. *Provocative Grace: The Challenge in Jesus' Words*. Nashville,
    TN: Upper Room Books, 2006.

Richards, D. A. J. *Why Love Leads to Justice: Love across the Boundaries*.
    New York: Cambridge University Press, 2016.

---

14   Ps. 46:1.

WHAT WILL YOU DO?

JIM WINKLER

Bishop W. Darin Moore, chair of the National Council of the Churches of Christ in the USA (NCC) Governing Board, began with an invitation to earnestly think, talk, and pray about the issue of racism and how it threatens the life and expressions of authentic Christianity. Other contributors and writers of *United Against Racism* took up matters of authentic Christianity, one that advocates that love, freedom, security, and peace are for all people of our nation and that God's creation opposes all forms of racial inequality and injustice. The question before us now is, What shall you and I do to end all negative thinking, harmful beliefs and behaviors, adverse actions, ineffective policies, and damaging practices that lead to racism? What will we do to continue and extend the work of Jesus Christ who lived, died, and was resurrected as a witness to the strength of love, the gift of freedom, the promise of security, and the power of peace—shalom that always works for reconciliation?

I believe that every person who claims to follow Jesus Christ must live like him. The NCC exists to embody this belief. The NCC exists to be known as "a community of communions called by Christ to visible unity and sent forth in the Spirit to promote God's justice, peace, and healing of the world."[1] Each and every day, in our homes and neighborhoods, at our places of work and worship, Christians are called to be agents of love, safety, and openness and advocates of freedom, justice, and equality. We are summoned to be persistent resisters against racism, inequality, and all forms of evil that oppress, marginalize, and inhibit God's creation from being all that God intends for it to be and become. In *United Against Racism,* the NCC convenes Christians—individually and collectively—to be authentic, genuine followers of Jesus.

---

1   From the National Council of Churches bylaws, adopted November 15, 2015.

For many years, I led seminars on social justice concerns for United Methodist youth, college students, and adults. Most of the participants were white, which is not surprising in that the United Methodist Church (TUMC) is a more than 90 percent white denomination. Quite a few of those seminars focused on racism, particularly after the uprising in Los Angeles following the Rodney King verdict.

It was as if suddenly white folks rediscovered racism in this country. The seminars featured bible study and worship; speakers; meetings on Capitol Hill; journeys into the Washington, DC, community; and simulation experiences.

I wanted to help these young people understand that racism is a system. Slavery was a system. Jim Crow was a system.

One of the most effective tools I used was Peggy McIntosh's "white privilege" toolkit. This was a list of some fifty statements such as the following:

- I can if I wish arrange to be in the company of people of my race most of the time.
- If I should need to move, I can be pretty sure of renting or purchasing housing in an area that I can afford and in which I would want to live.
- I can go shopping alone most of the time, pretty well assured that I will not be followed or harassed.
- I can turn on the television or look at the front page of the paper and see people of my race widely represented.
- When I am told about our national heritage or about "civilization," I am shown that people of my color made it what it is.
- I can be sure that my children will be given curricular materials that testify to the existence of their race.

We would form a circle, and each person would read a statement. By the end, the cumulative impact of more than fifty statements would begin to raise the consciousness of the young people present. Most of them had simply not thought about their privilege.

From that point, we would discuss the definition of racism, identified by the UMC as "power plus prejudice." This was hard for participants to grasp because they liked to insist that "anyone can be racist."

To incorporate the power dynamic into their thinking was challenging at best. I used facts, experiential methods, scripture, and anything else I could think of to help young people, mostly white, understand the depth and extent of racism in our society. I viewed it as missionary work.

I pointed out the negative health impact of racism such as higher blood pressure, higher rates of cancer, and lower rates of treatment for people of color.

I helped them understand the prevalence of negative media images. Recently, you'll recall that Dove Soap ran a racist ad in which a black American woman removes her shirt to reveal a "clean" white woman. I wanted my students to begin thinking critically about such things.

Many white people are fond of saying, "I don't see color," but a study showed that newly released white felons experience better job-hunting success than young black men with no criminal record.[2] Another famous experiment reveals applicants with Anglo-sounding names were 50 percent more likely to get calls for interviews than their counterparts who had black-sounding names.[3]

Enormously challenging aspects of work with white people of good will regarding racism, white supremacy, and white nationalism are issues of guilt and ignorance or naïveté. The weight of guilt sometimes blocks people from moving forward. I was part of a small dinner conversation some time ago with a group that included Congressman Emanuel Cleaver of Kansas City. He pointed out that whites define racism very narrowly and say, "I don't use the N word or I don't mind if they live next door." Clever described this type of racism as unconsciously

---

2   Devah Pager, "The Mark of a Criminal Record," *American Journal of Sociology* 108, no. 5 (2003): 937–75.

3   Marianne Bertrand and Sendhil Mullainathan, "Are Emily and Greg More Employable than Lakisha and Jamal? A Field Experiment of Labor Market Discrimination" (working paper 9873, July 2003), http://www.nber.org/papers/w9873.

rather than intentional. Such comments display a lack of understanding the distinction between personal prejudice and the systemic, structural character of racism—prejudice plus power, the authority to arrange relations and allocate resources based on privilege afforded by color.

Many whites have convinced themselves that white people suffer more discrimination than do blacks, but as Nicholas Kristof pointed out in an article in the *New York Times*, the US has a greater wealth gap between whites and blacks than South Africa had during apartheid.[4]

Many whites are quick to draw the race card and shut down when discussion of racism hits too close to home, but of course this isn't a card game. In what is referred to as a postfact, posttruth world, a whole lot of white people are going to deny the facts or ignore them, but not every one of us.

Recently I participated in a very diverse retreat of faith leaders. There was a great deal of lament expressed about our current national situation. In fact, I have been in a number of retreats since 2017 in which many people were very clear about how our nation was moving further and further away from being one nation under God as revealed through the legacy of love Jesus lived. But what will whites from pulpits, pews, churches, and community organizations do?

The National Council of Churches' November 2017 Church Unity Gathering theme was "Resistance, Resilience, and Persistence." Working for resilience is a concrete step people of good will can take to realize an authentic Christianity expressed in an inclusive, beloved community. Juliana McGene has documented that "positive social connections, when established, can provide important social resources that alter the way individuals experience and respond to stressful events or circumstances."[5] McGene describes four elements of positive social relationships

---

4   Nicholas Kristof, "When Whites Just Don't Get It: After Ferguson, Race Deserves More Attention, Not Less," *New York Times*, August 31, 2014, http://www.nytimes .com/2014/08/31/opinion/sunday/nicholas-kristof-after-ferguson-race-deserves -more-attention-not-less.html?smid=tw-share&_r=1.

5   Juliana McGene, *Social Fitness and Resilience: A Review of Relevant Constructs, Measures, and Links to Well-Being* (Santa Monica, CA: Rand Corporation, 2013), vii.

that promote resilience—emotional, instrumental, informational, and appraisal supports. Emotional support may be as simple and direct as having someone to talk with about one's concerns and challenges. Churches that acknowledge and demonstrate a willingness to confront racism provide fuel for resilience. Instrumental support might involve arranging transportation when needed or providing child or adult care that enables other household members to work. Too many people of color are unable to hold a job because they literally cannot get to work. Lack of transportation or affordable care for children or older adults living in the home are constant concerns of the unemployed. Informational support refers to providing awareness and knowledge about where opportunities exist; who provides competent, affordable services to address one's needs; where the safe houses in communities are located; and where the emphasis of law enforcers is not on keeping the peace but on locking up suspects. Appraisal supports are critical to the work of uniting against racism. These provide information and skills for self-evaluation and can extend to assess the value of other things—policies, programs, strategies, and tactics.[6] All four supports are distinct and interrelated.

Christians, individually and collectively, who work toward an inclusive, beloved community can take responsibility to provide these forms of support. Churches who work for change to overcome all forms of discrimination and racism can select and elect people to positions of religious and political leadership who understand and are committed to policies that rearrange current social patterns and allocate resources in ways that promote racial fairness and justice. Working for resiliency, Christians can ameliorate, if not alleviate, root causes and consequences of racism.

Metaphorically, we perceived the shift in the winds of time—shifts from a more loving, secure, and inclusive beloved community to a nation where many in power explicitly pitted neighbor against neighbor in efforts to promote an exclusive, closed society. We sensed it, and it is

---

6   McGene, 6–7.

coming. I don't know what else to do but keep on keeping on. Someone said recently that most all the kings of Israel and Judah in the Bible were scoundrels, but Jesus nevertheless proclaimed the reign of God.

The psalmist writes in Psalm 11,

> *In the Lord I take refuge; how can you say to me,*
> *"flee like a bird to the mountains;*
> *for look, the wicked bend the bow,*
> *they have fitted their arrow to the string,*
> *to shoot in the dark at the upright in heart.*
> *If the foundations are destroyed,*
> *what can the righteous do?"*
> *The Lord is in his holy temple;*
> *the Lord's throne is in heaven.*
> *His eyes behold, his gaze examines humankind.*
> *The Lord tests the righteous and the wicked,*
> *and his soul hates the lover of violence.*
> *On the wicked he will rain*
> *coals of fire and sulfur;*
> *a scorching wind shall be the portion of their cup.*
> *For the Lord is righteous;*
> *he loves righteous deeds;*
> *the upright shall behold his face.*

All I know to do is love the Lord and His righteous deeds and take refuge in the Lord. I know that a lot of us feel exhausted and frustrated. I know a lot of black American church leaders doubt the sincerity of the white church. There are many days I doubt the sincerity of the white church too.

I can't get many so-called white evangelical Christians to make common cause with us. So many of them are feeling triumphant right now. They have access, and they think that gives them power. I can't worry about them too much. What I can do is practice authentic Christianity, as I have come to know and understand Jesus as the ultimate advocate of love, freedom, security, and peace, truths that move the world toward the reconciliation Christ makes possible.

What the NCC Is Doing

I'm grateful that at the NCC, we have Bishop Darin Moore as our chairman. Bishop Moore brings a purposeful passion to the work of Christian unity with equity and justice. His has demonstrated on behalf of the NCC a skilled aptitude for combining missional focus and fiscal accountability. I'm grateful we are pushing forward on a racial justice truth-telling initiative.

The racial justice truth-telling initiative of the National Council of Churches builds on many years of commitment to equality, justice, and civil rights. As white supremacy and white nationalism reemerge from the cover of night, the NCC commits to proving social supports for victims of racism, to awakening the souls of American churches to God's vision for creation, to confronting the legislative policies and economic powerful for an equitable distribution of resources, to pressing for the transformation of society so that liberty and justice can be experienced by all—to realizing Dr. Martin Luther King's vision of a beloved community. The NCC is not perfect, but we are a diverse national ecumenical organization.

Our racial justice truth-telling initiative is cochaired by Mrs. Jacqueline Dupont Walker, executive director of the African Methodist Episcopal Church Social Action Commission, and Rev. John Dorhauer, general minister and president of the United Church of Christ. At first, we thought of this as a truth and reconciliation process—perhaps similar to those in South Africa, Brazil, and Guatemala—but we concluded quickly that the white church likes to move straight to reconciliation and pass over truth.

This initiative is unfolding in the context of the United Nations' International Decade for People of African Descent, of which there are more than two hundred million in the Americas, and following a visit last year of a delegation of church leaders from around the world who came to the US under the auspices of the World Council of Churches.

Our task force and our governing board have declared that our intention is to end racism. We decided not to mess around with lesser goals. It's time now to end racism, and we have faith that with God's help this can be done.

On April 4, 2018, the NCC will hold an interfaith worship service at the Lincoln Memorial in the morning. In the afternoon, we will gather thousands of people on the National Mall. The ACT Now: United to End Racism rally is the launch event of a multiyear initiative. The rally is cosponsored by a wide span of faith groups and will feature speakers and music. ACT Now: Unite to End Racism begins on the occasion of the Rev. Dr. Martin Luther King Jr.'s assassination. And in the evening, we will meet in the National Museum of African American History and Culture. We know and we are grateful many people will be in Memphis on April 4.

Going forward, the NCC hopes to work with leaders of good will and their organizations to influence policies to redress racism, to gather and organize networks of support and advocacy, and to implement measureable plans to erase racism from the face of our nation. We ask for your prayers and support.

Dr. King pointed out that our fate, the fate of black and white Americans, is inextricably bound together. I hope in the days, months, and years to come, you will resolve to live, and if necessary, die giving witness to authentic Christianity. The time is now, the spirit is real, and we are called.

God never promised the way forward would be easy. The Bible is full of stories of unlikely faithful people pushing forward in the midst of injustice—prostitutes, murderers, and thieves emerge as heroes. It might be that even the NCC can play a role in the struggle for God's justice and peace.

Our country is in a dark night of the soul. Last week I heard a Catholic priest say that the fact sexism, racism, patriotism, classism, nationalism, and homophobia have lasted this long indicates we are still living in early Christianity.

I do know that Jesus always takes the side of the outsider: the Samaritan, the Syrophoenician woman, and the Roman centurion. Jesus always liberates those without power.

Today, our nation is seemingly rooted in fear. But Dr. King reminded us that "the time is always right to do what's right."[7]

I believe that in the midst of all the pain and suffering we see around us, we have made progress, and we who follow Christ are a principal reason for that progress. But if our children and grandchildren will have a decent future, it will be because we changed the very direction of the United States to one committed to cooperation, justice, and peace. I am grateful to be in that struggle.

United Against Racism is a call to authentic Christianity. It summons Christians to pray, think, and act to end racism. Our hope is to help resource and support churches, communions, and those who endeavor to share the journey of the Christian faith in the pursuit of an unfinished agenda to embody a more excellent way of racial equity. Racial equity and authentic Christian faith are inextricably tied together.

---

7   Martin Luther King Jr.'s speech on "The Future of Integration," Oberlin University, October 22, 1964.

Learning Practices for People of Faith

Mary E. Hess, PhD

"Seeing Through" Popular Media

In the summer of 2016, in the heat of the US presidential campaign, the president of Union Seminary published an essay in *Time* titled "How to Heal the Spiritual Pain of America."[1] Her essay was focused on the stories we tell in the United States about ourselves as a nation and asked us to remember that

> there is no religious or spiritual tradition, at least any worth their salt, that does not begin with a serious account of both the good and bad that people can do. There are many names for the negative side of human existence, such as sin, evil, illusion, moral absence, iniquity, transgression and negative karma. All recognize that human beings, alone and collectively, can do really bad things. This doesn't mean we don't have a good side. But these stories insist that if we do not existentially reckon with the ugly side of our beliefs and actions, we will not have healthy communities. Egregious harms will continue to unfold and profound despair and alienation inevitably set in. Why? Because deep down, we are living a spiritual lie.

I have a hunch that this spiritual lie is something that many people who are leaving religious communities have sensed and cannot endure. What is heartbreaking, however, is precisely Jones's point: that communities of faith have profound convictions about human brokenness and vital sources for engaging in reconciliation and healing.

---

1   Serene Jones, "How to Heal the Spiritual Pain of America," *Time*, September 7, 2016, http://time.com/4477582/heal-the-spiritual-pain-of-america/.

In the United States we are inhabiting in 2018, we have to struggle with context and with the challenges of context collapse. We are learning, as never before, how much our context shapes how we see the world. The stories we tell ourselves, the stories we allow ourselves to hear, differ dramatically depending on where we live, who we count as our neighbors, let alone who we fear. But it is not simply our context that matters; it is also that our contexts are collapsing all around us. We cannot count on listening to the same music, watching the same films, and eating the same foods as ways to know each other. Even when we try to share these things often, they have been ripped out of their original settings and floated on a digital sea, making them harder to understand and easier to *misunderstand*.

Day after day, moment to moment, people experience in digital media a connection, a relationship of shared meaning, of shared resonance, even (for many) a community. But are we finding ways to invite the stranger into our relationships, into our communities? Are we open to seeing how estranged we have become from much of who we really are (in the deep sense of shared communion)? Are we open to the wisdom of our tradition that might actually be found, or at least connected to, in the midst of digital media?

For many of us, the term *reconciliation* has very little meaning. What little meaning does exist is often captured, in economic terms, as the "reconciliation of accounts" that occurs in a bookkeeper's office or that entails ensuring consistency across spreadsheets. But that very narrow definition is far from being the primary meaning of the word. Even dictionaries list several others first—the "restoration of friendly relations" or "the action of making one view or belief compatible with another."[2]

In Christian terms, reconciliation is the very heart of the Gospel, the very heart of all that the Incarnation accomplishes. Remember the quote from Serene Jones: to heal America's spiritual pain, we must acknowledge our brokenness and seek healing. This path is what Christianity is all about, no matter how warped or deformed it has become in the

---

2   MacOS dictionary.

intervening two millennia since Jesus gathered a community committed to reconciliation.

Schreiter defines reconciliation as "the work of God"[3] and notes the following:

- "God begins the reconciling process with the healing of the victim."[4]
- "The healing process in reconciliation makes of the victim (and the healed wrongdoer) a 'new creation.'"[5]
- "A path towards reconciliation requires finding a way to cope with suffering."[6]
- "Reconciliation will only be complete when God has reconciled the whole universe in Christ."[7]

Schreiter continues by suggesting that the principal practices of reconciliation are the following:

- healing (of memories, victims, and wrongdoers)
- truth-telling
- the pursuit of justice (punitive, restorative, structural)
- forgiveness[8]

Reconciliation Is at the Heart of the Gospel

Until we acknowledge pain, we cannot begin healing. Christ on the cross is the very heart of Christian community, but how often have we averted our eyes—not only from the cross, but from the deep pain in our midst? There is significant evidence that young people are not only

---

3   Robert Schreiter, "Reconciliation and Prophetic Dialogue," in *Mission on the Road to Emmaus: Constants, Context and Prophetic Dialogue*, ed. C. Ross and S. Bevans (Maryknoll, NY: Orbis Books, 2015).

4   Ross and Bevans, *Mission on the Road to Emmaus*, 127.

5   Ross and Bevans, 127.

6   Ross and Bevans, 128.

7   Ross and Bevans, 128.

8   Ross and Bevans, 129–32.

open to the pain of the world but energized by engaging it and seeking healing.[9] There is also significant evidence that they are motivated and encouraged by the social media they consume—including even the video games they play.[10]

What can it look like to begin appreciatively in "believing" as a way toward reconciliation? It looks like hospitality; it looks like learning a way of attending or practicing attention, which invites room for deep listening. Very few of us have any practice with this kind of listening. It takes support and structure to enter such a process. The good news is that dozens of organizations have woken up to this challenge and are offering support and tools for doing so.

All these projects begin by helping groups form shared agreements about how their conversation will proceed. The Forum for Theological Exploration has such an agreement, as does the Minnesota Respectful Conversations Project (see the end of this chapter). These agreements help people by giving them an "etiquette" or set of guidelines to help a conversation move forward. The key is that such conversations are not about changing people's minds; they are not about debating ideas but rather about seeking understanding and in doing so opening up people's hearts.[11]

Four-Person Story Circle

One of my favorite such exercises is the four-person story circle. You begin this practice by dividing people into groups of four and then explaining that each person in the group will have a particular task and that these tasks will rotate until every person in the group has had the opportunity to try each one. The exercise then moves to asking one person to tell a story—

---

9   R. Hutt, "What Do Young People Value?," *World Economic Forum*, 2016, https://www.weforum.org/agenda/2016/01/what-do-young-people-value/.

10   See the central argument in J. McGonigal, *Reality Is Broken: Why Games Make Us Better and How They Can Change the World* (New York: Random House, 2011).

11   See Parker Palmer's central arguments in his book, *Healing the Heart of Democracy: The Courage to Create a Politics Worthy of the Human Heart* (San Francisco: Jossey-Bass, 2014).

keeping it short, timed to no more than three minutes. You can ask for stories about any number of experiences (tell us about a time you caught a glimpse of love, tell us about a time that you experienced surprise, tell us about a time you felt healing, and so on). While the storyteller is sharing her story, the other three people in the group listen carefully in three ways: one listens for any *feelings* expressed in the story, one listens for any *actions* expressed in the story, and one listens for any *values* expressed in the story. Once the storyteller is finished, the other three listeners share what they have heard. After a short pause, the tasks rotate one person over (so the storyteller now becomes a story listener, the person listening for feelings now listens for actions, and so on). Once all four people have had a chance to try each task, the small group joins other small groups to process the experience together.

This is an example of a structure, a set of "rules," if you will, that helps create a space in which people are focused on listening carefully.

Story Titling

Another example is what I call a "story-titling" exercise. Much like the previous example, this is geared toward a small group and toward listening to a story. In this case, it's important to ensure that you have someone who can time what is going on—most people use a phone alarm set to three minutes. Here one person tells a story and then physically turns around so that she is not facing the other three people. At that point the listeners offer possible titles for the story. The storyteller listens to these possible titles, all the while *not* looking at the listeners. Then the storyteller turns around and chooses one of the titles or offers one that she has made up and prefers herself. The group writes down the title, and then the next person tells a story, and the process is repeated. When everyone has had a chance to tell a story and have it "titled," the list of titles becomes a "table of contents" for the group and can be shared in a larger group setting.

In this exercise, both the timing and the process of not watching the faces of people offering titles are important. And for both of these exercises—the story circle and the story titling—I've found that it helps to remind people that sometimes it's difficult to come up with a story and that it's fine for a person to "pass" on telling a story. It's also important to remind people that these are stories for telling, not for fixing, and even less for doubting and contradicting—that is, the goal is to listen carefully to a story, not to try to be a counselor or an advocate but simply a good listener.

Stories through Digital Media

The final example I want to use connects the bones and flesh of our religious beliefs with the fluid and rapidly changing stories of digital media. This example draws on the classic work of Patricia O'Connell Killen, who along with John de Beer expressed a practice for reflections about God back in the early nineties that has proven remarkably fruitful even as our contexts have shifted and changed.[12] Her process invites participants to walk through a series of prompts and, in doing so, to perceive connections between their own experiences and those of scripture and tradition. I recommend her book,[13] as she goes into much greater depth than I can and offers many versions of the process.

In this exercise, I show a television commercial three times. First, I invite participants to view it once without doing anything other than experiencing it. The second and third times, I ask them to pay attention to what they are feeling (both physically and emotionally) as they watch it. I have done this in several ways—sometimes asking people to respond to questions in pairs, sometimes asking them to think about and write down their own responses. I ask them questions that use Killen's language: What is existence like in this commercial? What is joyful in it? What is broken or sorrowing about it? Are there possibilities for newness and healing present? These questions raise key theological themes but without using explicitly theological language.

Once people have had a chance to share how they have experienced the commercial in these ways, I ask them to think about whether there

---

12   See Patricia O'Connel Killen's book-length description in P. Killen and John de Beer, *The Art of Theological Reflection* (New York: Crossroad, 1994).

13   Killen and de Beer.

are any biblical stories, prayers, or hymns that this commercial story reminds them of. It's important not to press too hard on the possible resonances and to make sure that people understand there is no "right or wrong" answer here, only what emerges for them. If they can think of some examples, I ask them to go and find that passage, hymn, or prayer and think about it again, to pay attention to all that it is saying and especially to think about it in light of what they are feeling with the commercial. Killen's process invites people to then think about what actions such resonances invite—I love that question! But since I am often doing this in a setting where there is only an hour or so for our process, that is usually a prompt I use as a "sending" question at the close of our time.

Television commercials—at least the ones with which I practice this exercise—are beautifully produced short-form narratives. They are very effective at eliciting some form of desire, some kind of yearning, which their audience might reasonably expect to exhibit. I think it is generative to help people to name the yearning they feel the commercial has invited and then to identify a deeper response than whatever "product" the commercial is attempting to salve that yearning through. I use the word "salve" quite intentionally, because it has been my experience that commercials quite often subtly "promise" a certain kind of "salvation" through purchase. I want to support a different form of action all together, one that recognizes God's agency.

Commercial Examples to Use

I collect commercials that are useful for this exercise at my research site, StoryingFaith.org (http://www.storyingfaith.org/archives/780). Here are several that I have found to work well in the contexts in which I generally teach:

> Adidas, "Break Free" (https://youtu.be/gXfLl3qYy0k)
> Amazon Prime (https://youtu.be/hKEzqGHS2hw)
> Android, "Be Together, Not the Same" (https://youtu.be/AD
> -oCSoI9OQ)

Apple, "The Human Family" (https://youtu.be/E5S5ZmC-5HI)

Apple, "Misunderstood" (https://youtu.be/v76f6KPSJ2w)

Apple, "The Song" (https://youtu.be/N2ubgxn8aQ8)

Barbie, "Imagine the Possibilities" (https://youtu.be/l1vnsqbnAkk)

Danish TV2 (https://youtu.be/jD8tjhVO1Tc)

Heineken, "Worlds Apart" (https://youtu.be/8wYXw4K0A3g)

Honey Maid, "This Is Wholesome" (https://youtu.be/2xeanX6xnRU)

Nike, "Equality" (https://youtu.be/43QTjFCPLtI)

Nike, "Together" (https://youtu.be/n6S1JoCSVNU)

Oreo, "Dare to Wonder" (https://www.youtube.com/watch?v=IQNAVLsvFjI)

Pepsi, "Forever Young" (https://youtu.be/tLfrdRgpKfI)

President's Choice (Canada) (https://www.youtube.com/watch?v=vDuA9OPyp6I)

State Farm, "Following" (https://youtu.be/VuyhmA5YAu8)

TIAA, "This Is Success" (https://youtu.be/5DeQMbC1P2U)

2016 Chevrolet mascots (https://youtu.be/U5rxkuaYHpU)

YouTube Music, "Afsa's Song" (https://youtu.be/WO1r5jHrOuE)

You can also do this exercise with public service announcements:

Always, "Like a Girl" (https://youtu.be/XjJQBjWYDTs)

Dove, "Real Beauty Sketches" (https://youtu.be/litXW91UauE)

Dove, "Selfie" (https://youtu.be/_3agBWqGfRo)

Perception (https://youtu.be/A8syQeFtBKc)

Wishes (https://youtu.be/ON6hAudgqMg)

Extended Readings

History and Race Politics

Diop, Cheikh Anta, and Harold Salemson. *Precolonial Black Africa*. Chicago: Lawrence Hill Books, 1987.

Higginbotham, A. Leon, Jr. *Shades of Freedom: Racial Politics and Presumptions of the American Legal Process*. Oxford University Press, 1996.

Marable, Manning. *Race, Reform, and Rebellion: The Second Reconstruction and Beyond in Black America, 1945–2006*. 3rd ed. University of Mississippi Press, 2007.

Culture and African American Christianity

Boesak, Allan Aubrey, and Curtiss Paul DeYoung. *Radical Reconciliation: Beyond Political Pietism and Christian Quietism*. Maryknoll, NY: Orbis Books, 2012.

Carter, J. Kameron. *Race: A Theological Account*. Oxford University Press, 2008.

Grant, Jacqueline. *White Women's Christ and Black Women's Jesus: Feminist Christology and Womanist Response*. American Academy of Religion Academy Series, edited by Susan Thistlewaite, no. 64. Atlanta, GA: Scholars Press, 1989.

Hopkins, Dwight N. *Being Human: Race Culture and Religion*. Fortress, 2005.

Jennings, Willie James. *The Christian Imagination: Theology and Origins of Race*. Yale University Press, 2010.

Whelchel, L. H., Jr. *The History and Heritage of African-American Churches: A Way Out of No Way*. St. Paul, MN: Paragon House, 2011.

Race Pedagogy

Bonilla-Silva, Eduardo. *Racism without Racists: Color-Blind Racism & Racial Inequality in Contemporary America*. Rowman & Littlefield, 2010.

Davies, Susan E. *Ending Racism in the Church.* Cleveland, OH: United Church Press, 1998.

DiAngelo, Robin. *What Does It Mean to Be White? Developing White Racial Literacy.* New York: Peter Lang, 2012.

Douglas, Kelly Brown. *Stand Your Ground: Black Bodies and the Justice of God.* Maryknoll, NY: Orbis Books, 2015.

Evans, Joseph. *Lifting the Veil over Eurocentrism.* Africa World Press, 2014.

Harvey, Jennifer. *Dear White Christians: For Those Still Longing for Racial Reconciliation.* Grand Rapids, MI: William B. Eerdmans, 2014.

Robinson, Elaine A. *Race and Theology (Horizons in Theology).* Abingdon Press, 2012.

Rothenberg, Paula S. *White Privilege: Essential Readings on the Other Side of Racism.* 4th ed. Worth, 2011.

Sue, Derald Wing. *Race Talk and the Conspiracy of Silence: Understanding and Facilitating Difficult Dialogues on Race.* Hoboken, NJ: Wiley, 2015.

Tochluk, Shelly. *Witnessing Whiteness: The Need to Talk about Race and How to Do It.* Rowman & Littlefield, 2010.

Unander, Dave. *Shattering the Myth of Race: Genetic Realities and Biblical Truths.* Valley Forge, PA: Judson Press, 2000.

Vitalis, Robert. *White World Order, Black Power Politics: The Birth of American International Relations.* Ithaca, NY: Cornell University Press, 2015.

Biblical and Theological Resources
Blount, Brian K., and Cain Hope Felder, eds. *True to Our Native Land: An African American New Testament Commentary.* Minneapolis, MN: Fortress, 2007.

Felder, Cain Hope, ed. *Stony the Road We Trod: African American Biblical Interpretation.* Minneapolis, MN: Fortress, 1991.

Page, Hugh R., Jr., ed. *The Africana Bible: Reading Israel's Scriptures from Africa and the African Diaspora.* Minneapolis, MN: Fortress, 2010.

Williams, Delores S. *Sisters in the Wilderness: The Challenges of Womanist God-Talk.* Maryknoll, NY: Orbis Books, 2005.

Selected Readings

Coates, Ta-Nehisi. "The Case for Reparations." *Atlantic,* May 21, 2014.

Hayner, Patricia B. *Unspeakable Truths: Facing the Challenge of Truth Commissions.* London: Routledge, 2002.

Newcomb, Steve. *The Doctrine of Discovery.* http://www.doctrineof discovery.org/.

Perkinson, James. *White Theology: Outing Supremacy in Modernity (Black Religion/Womanist Thought/Social Justice).* New York: Palgrave Macmillan, 2004.

Articles and DVD Resources

Boyce, Gregory. "The Execution of Michael Brown: A Barbershop Analysis of a Police-Murder." *Examiner,* December 2, 2014. http://www.examiner.com/article/the-execution-of-michael-brown-a-barbershopanalysis.

Coates, Ta-Nehisi. "The Case for Reparations." *Atlantic,* June 2014. http://www.theatlantic.com/magazine/archive/2014/06/the-case-for-reparations/361631/.

Cobb, Jelani. "Murders in Charleston." *New Yorker,* June 18, 2015. http://www.newyorker.com/news/news-desk/church-shooting-charleston-southcarolina.

Franklin, Neil. "Bias Is Universal. Awareness Can Assure Justice." *New York Times,* September 2, 2014. http://www.nytimes.com/roomfordebate/2014/09/01/black-and-white-and-blue/bias-isuniversal-awareness-can-assure-justice.

Herbes-Sommers, Christine, dir. *Race: The Power of an Illusion.* California Newsreel, 2003. DVD.

CONTRIBUTORS

Prayer Contributors
Rev. Donald H. Ashmall
Council Minister
International Council of Community Churches

His Eminence Archbishop Vicken Aykazian
Diocesan Legate and Director of the Ecumenical Office
Diocese of the Armenian Church in America

Bishop George E. Battle Jr.
Senior Bishop
African Methodist Episcopal Zion Church
Presiding Prelate of the Piedmont Episcopal District

Min. Tanya Boucicaut
Millennial in the Baptist tradition

Rev. Kathryn Brown, Secretary
Christian Education Department
African Methodist Episcopal Zion Church

Rev. Randy Creath
Musician, Writer, Pastor without fences

The Most Rev. Michael Bruce Curry
XXVII Presiding Bishop
The Episcopal Church

The Rev. Paula Clayton Dempsey
Director of Partnership Relations
Alliance of Baptists in the USA

The Rev. Dr. John C. Dorhauer
General Minister and President
United Church of Christ

The Rev. Elizabeth A. Eaton
Presiding Bishop
Evangelical Lutheran Church in America

Charles R. Foster
Professor of Religion and Education Emeritus
Candler School of Theology
Emory University

Rev. Ebony Grisom
American Baptist Church

Janné C. Grover
Apostle, Center USA Mission Field
Team Lead, Disciple and Priesthood Formation

Dr. Mary E. Hess
Professor of Educational Leadership
Luther Seminary

The Rev. Lauren Holder
St. Luke's Episcopal Church

Rev. Dr. Christian Iosso
Coordinator, Advisory Committee on Social Witness Policy
Presbyterian Mission Agency, Presbyterian Church (USA)

Rev. Dr. Denise Janssen
Associate Professor of Christian Education
Samuel D. Proctor School of Theology
Virginia Union University

Bishop Teresa E. Jefferson-Snorton
Presiding Prelate Fifth Episcopal District
Christian Methodist Episcopal Church

Rev. L. Callid Keefe-Perry
Educator, Minister, and Advocate for the Arts

Randy G. Litchfield
Professor in the Browning Chair of Christian Education
Director of Assessment
Methodist Theological School in Ohio

Kathryn Mary Lohre
Assistant to the Presiding Bishop
Executive, Ecumenical and Inter-religious Relations and Theological
    Discernment
Evangelical Lutheran Church in America

Rev. Donté McCutchen
Baptist Pastor
Love Cathedral Community Church

The Rev. Dr. Russell L. Meyer
Executive Director Florida Council of Churches

Mary Elizabeth Moore
Dean and Professor of Theology and Education
Boston University School of Theology

The Rt. Rev. W. Darin Moore
Presiding Prelate of the Mid-Atlantic Episcopal District
African Methodist Episcopal Zion Church

Rev. Teresa "Terri" Hord Owens
General Minister and President
Christian Church (Disciples of Christ)

Rev. Garland F. Pierce
Executive Director, Department of Christian Education
African Methodist Episcopal Church

Rev. Dr. W. Franklyn Richardson
Senior Pastor
Grace Baptist Church

The Rev'd Margaret R. Rose
Presiding Bishop's Deputy for Ecumenical and Inter-religious
    Relations
The Episcopal Church

Rev. Vernon Shannon
Ecumenical and Governmental Representative
Philadelphia and Baltimore African Methodist Episcopal Church
    (AME) Zion Church Conference

Jane Siebert
President
General Convention of the Swedenborgian Church of North
    America

Rev. Sheldon W. Sorge, PhD
General Minister
The Presbytery of Pittsburgh, Presbyterian Church (USA)

Rev. Albert Starr Jr.
Evangelical Lutheran Church in America
Director, Ethnic Specific and Multicultural Ministries
Program Director, African Descent Ministries

The Rev. Kevin L. Strickland
Assistant to the Presiding Bishop/Executive for Worship
Office of the Presiding Bishop
Evangelical Lutheran Church in America

Rev. Karen Georgia A. Thompson
Minister for Ecumenical and Interfaith Relations
United Church of Christ

The Rev. Jeffery L. Tribble Sr., PhD
South Atlantic Episcopal District Director of Continuing Education
The African Methodist Episcopal Zion Church

Rev. Dr. Angelique Walker-Smith
Senior Associate for Pan African and Orthodox Church Engagement
Bread for the World

Rev. Dr. Sharon Watkins
Christian Church (Disciples of Christ)

Bishop B. Michael Watson
The United Methodist Church

Rev. Dr. Nathaniel D. West
Director of the Master in Arts in Christian Education
Director of Formation and Counseling
Assistant Professor of Christian Education
Samuel Dewitt Proctor School of Theology
Virginia Union University

Rev. Nancy Lynne Westfield, PhD
Professor of Religious Education
Drew University Theological School

Rev. Dr. Tammy Wiens
Associate for Christian Formation
National Office of the Presbyterian Church (USA)

Bishop Sylvester Williams Sr.
Presiding Prelate, Third Episcopal District
Christian Methodist Episcopal Church

Jim Winkler
General Secretary and President
National Council of Churches

Rev. Janet L. Wolf
Director
Alex Haley Farm and Nonviolent Organizing
Children's Defense Fund

Rev. Dr. Mary H. Young
Director, Leadership Education
Association of Theological Schools

Rev. Dr. Christopher L. Zacharias
John Wesley AME Zion Church

Special Acknowledgments
Dr. Mitzi J. Budde
Head Librarian and Professor
Bishop Payne Library
Virginia Theological Seminary

Dr. Rex M. Ellis
Associate Director for Curatorial Affairs
National Museum of African American History and Culture
(NMAAHC) at the Smithsonian Institution

Dr. Mary E. Hess
Professor of Educational Leadership
Luther Seminary

The Rev. Karen Georgia A. Thompson
Minister for Ecumenical and Interfaith Relations
United Church of Christ

Participating and Referenced Communions and Organizations
African Methodist Episcopal Church[1] (AME Church) began in Philadelphia, Pennsylvania, in 1787, when persons in St. George's Methodist Episcopal Church withdrew in protest of racial segregation in the sanctuary. In 1816, led by Rev. Richard Allen, who had been ordained a deacon by Bishop Francis Asbury, the communion was officially formed.

African Methodist Episcopal Zion Church (AMEZ Church) became an independent body after members withdrew from John Street Methodist Church of New York City in 1796. James Varick was consecrated as its first bishop.

Alliance of Baptists, founded in 1987, is an association of individuals and churches dedicated to the preservation of historic Baptist principles, freedoms, and traditions and to the expression of ministry and mission through cooperative relationships (http://www.allianceofbaptists.org).

---

1   All information on participating and referenced religious bodies is provided courtesy of the National Council of the Churches of Christ in the USA and is from the Eileen W. Linder, ed., *Yearbook of American & Canadian Churches 2012* (Nashville, TN: Abingdon, 2012).

American Baptist Churches in the USA, originally known as Northern Baptist Convention, is committed to holding the name in trust for all Christians of like faith and mind who desire to bear witness to the historical Baptist convictions in a framework of cooperative Protestantism. American Baptist work at the local level has affinity to the witness of Roger Williams of the First Baptist Church in Providence, Rhode Island, in 1638 (http://www.abc-usa.org).

Armenian Apostolic Church, Diocese of America, began in AD 301, at the foot of the biblical Mount Ararat in the ancient land of Armenia, where two of Christ's holy apostles, Saints Thaddeus and Bartholomew, preached Christianity in the first century. Today, the Armenian Apostolic Church of America operates though eastern and western dioceses (http://www.armenianchurch.org).

Christian Church (Disciples of Christ) in the United States and Canada began in the early 1800s on the American frontier, led by Thomas and Alexander Campbell in western Pennsylvania and Barton W. Stone in Kentucky. The Christian Church (Disciples of Christ) claims no official doctrine but operates within strong, voluntary covenantal ties to one another (http://www.disciples.org).

Christian Methodist Episcopal Church (CME Church) is a historic African American communion that began in 1870 in Jackson, Tennessee. Organized by former enslaved persons from eight annual conferences of the Methodist Episcopal Church South, they were initially named the Colored Methodist Episcopal Church in America. Officially changing the name to Christian Methodist Episcopal Church in 1956, the education of African Americans has been one of its most notable hallmarks (http://www.thecmechurch.org).

Community of Christ was founded in 1830 and is present in almost fifty nations with about 250,000 members worldwide. Its mission is to proclaim Jesus Christ and promote communities of joy, hope, love, and peace. Their priesthood includes both men and women (http://www.CofChrist.org).

Episcopal Church entered the colonies with early settlers at Jamestown, Virginia, in 1607 as the Church of England. The Episcopal

Church became an autonomous body after the Revolutionary War in 1789 as the Protestant Episcopal Church in the United States of America. The Episcopal Church, like Catholic and Reformed traditions, regard apostolic succession and the historic creeds of Christendom as essential elements of faith and order as well as the primacy of Holy Scripture and the sacraments of baptism and Eucharist (http://www.episcopalchurch.org).

Evangelical Lutheran Church of America (ELCA) was organized April 30–May 3, 1987, in Columbus, Ohio, with the union of the American Lutheran Church, the Lutheran Church of America, and the Association of Evangelical Lutheran Churches. The ELCA was a founding member of the Lutheran World Federation, the World Council of Churches, and the National Council of the Churches of Christ in the USA (http://www.elca.org).

International Council of Community Churches (ICCC), established in 1950, is a fellowship of locally autonomous, ecumenically minded, congregationally governed, noncreedal churches. The body is a result of a union of black churches known as the Biennial Council of Community Churches in the United States and Elsewhere and white churches known as the National Council of Community Churches (www.icccnow.org).

National Council of the Churches of Christ in the USA has served as a leading voice of witness to the living Christ since 1950. NCC unifies a diverse covenant community of thirty-eight member communions and more than forty million individuals—100,000 congregations from Protestant, Anglican, Orthodox, Evangelical, historic African American, and Living Peace traditions—in a common commitment to advocate and represent God's love and promise of unity in our public square. NCC partners with secular and interfaith partners to advance a shared agenda of peace, progress, and positive change (http://nationalcouncilofchurches.us).

Presbyterian Church (USA) was organized June 10, 1983, when the Presbyterian Church in the United States and the United Presbyterian Church in the United States of America united in Atlanta. The union healed a major division that began with the Civil War when Presbyterians in the South withdrew from the Presbyterian Church in the United States of America to form the Presbyterian Church in the Confederate States (http://www.pcusa.org).

Progressive National Baptist Convention Inc. was organized in November 1961 in Cincinnati, Ohio. Founder L. Venchael Booth, Martin Luther King Jr., and other black Baptist leaders committed to be a progressive Christian African American body in the Baptist tradition to emphasize civil rights and social justice. The membership continues to appreciate political activism that is informed by shared understandings of "fellowship, progress, service, and peace."[2]

Swedenborgian Church was founded in America in 1792 as the Church of the New Jerusalem. The church affirms freedom of choice as persons follow life's path experiencing both good and evil. Swedenborgian tradition is a biblically based theology derived from the spiritual or mystical experiences and exhaustive biblical studies of the Swedish scientist and philosopher Emanuel Swedenborg (1688–1772; http://www.swedenborg.org).

United Church of Christ (UCC) was constituted on June 25, 1957, by representatives of the Congregational Christian Churches and of the Evangelical and Reformed Church in Cleveland, Ohio. The preamble to UCC's constitution includes an acknowledgment of Jesus Christ as its sole head and as kindred in Christ all who share in this confession (http://www.ucc.org).

The United Methodist Church was formed on April 23, 1968, with the union of the Methodist Church and the Evangelical United Brethren Church, which shared a common historical and spiritual heritage. The Methodist movement began in eighteenth-century England under the preaching of John Wesley. The Christmas Conference in Baltimore, Maryland, in 1784 marks the establishment of the ecclesial

---

2   Albert A. Avant Jr., *Social Teaching of the Progressive National Baptist Convention, Inc., since 1961: A Critical Analysis of the Least, the Lost, and the Left-Out* (New York: Routledge, 2003).

organization in the colonies where Francis Asbury was elected as its first bishop (http://www.umc.org).

Editorial Team

Rev. Kathryn Brown, Secretary
Christian Education Department
African Methodist Episcopal Zion Church

Janné C. Grover, Apostle
Central USA Mission Field
Team Lead, Disciples and Priesthood Formation
Community of Christ

Rev. Dr. Velda R. Love
Minister for Racial Justice
United Church of Christ
Justice and Witness Ministries

Rev. Garland F. Pierce
Executive Director
Department of Christian Education
African Methodist Episcopal Church

Toya Richards
Communications Specialist
Alliance of Baptists

Rev. Karen Georgia Thompson
United Church of Christ

Rev. Dr. Jeffery L. Tribble Sr.
Associate Professor of Ministry
Columbia Theological Seminary

Project Consultants
Minister Tanya Y. Boucicaut
Virginia Commonwealth University

Dr. Tony Kireopoulos
Associate General Secretary
National Council of Churches

About the Press

Friendship Press hosts conversations that matter, informed by the life and teachings of Jesus. The Press gives voice to ideas for living with purpose. Friendship Press helps leaders develop essential resources to support the vision, values, and practices of their community.

Joining and supporting leaders and communities help Friendship Press achieve its mission of pursuing peace, seeking justice, caring for the earth, and fostering communities of love, hope, and reconciliation.

Friendship Press
an affiliate of the National Council of Churches
Conversations that Matter